Passport's Illustrated Guide to
BUDAPEST

SECOND EDITION

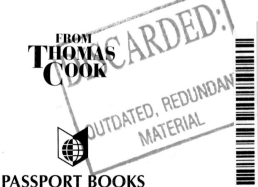

FROM
THOMAS
COOK

PASSPORT BOOKS
NTC/Contemporary Publishing Group

HUNGARY

This edition first published in 2000 by Passport Books
A division of NTC/Contemporary Publishing Group, Inc.
4255 West Touhy Avenue
Lincolnwood (Chicago), Illinois
60712–1975 U.S.A.

Written by Louis James
Original photography by Ken Patterson

Edited, designed, and produced by AA Publishing.
© The Automobile Association 1995, 2000.
Maps © The Automobile Association 1995, 2000.
First published 1995
Reprinted 1996
Revised second edition 2000

Library of Congress Catalog Card Number: on file

ISBN 0-658-00147-7

The contents of this publication are believed correct at the time of printing.
Nevertheless the publishers cannot accept responsibility for any errors or
omissions, for changes in the details given in this guide, or for the
consequences of any reliance on the information provided by the same.
Assessments of attractions, hotels, restaurants, and so forth are based upon
the author's own experience and therefore descriptions given in this guide
necessarily contain an element of subjective opinion that may not reflect the
publisher's opinion or dictate a reader's own experiences on another occasion.
**We have tried to ensure accuracy in this guide, but things do
change and we would be grateful if readers would advise us of any
inaccuracies they may encounter.**

Published by Passport Books in conjunction with AA Publishing and the
Thomas Cook Group Ltd.

Color separation: BTB Colour Reproduction, Whitchurch, Hampshire,
England.

Printed by: Edicoes ASA, Oporto, Portugal.

Cover photographs: front, copyright © John Gottberg/Dave G. Houser
Stock Photography; spine © Dave G. Houser.

Contents

About this Book

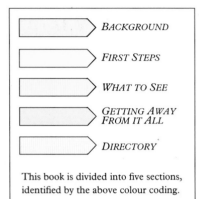

> BACKGROUND

> FIRST STEPS

> WHAT TO SEE

> GETTING AWAY FROM IT ALL

> DIRECTORY

This book is divided into five sections, identified by the above colour coding.

Background gives an introduction to the city – its history, geography, politics, culture.
First Steps offers practical advice on arriving and getting around.
What to See is an alphabetical listing of places to visit, with walks.

Getting Away From it All highlights places off the beaten track where you can relax and enjoy peace and quiet.
Finally, the **Directory** provides practical information – from shopping and entertainment to children and sport, including a section on business matters. Special highly illustrated features on specific aspects of the city appear throughout the book.

TELEPHONE NUMBERS
Every effort has been made to ensure telephone numbers are correct, but these do change frequently. If you have difficulty in dialling a number please ring 198 for domestic enquiries and 199 for international enquiries. Be aware, however, that domestic operators may not speak English.

The tomb of the poet Endre Ady (facing page)

BACKGROUND

'This people is full of
ingenuity, ability, talent
and vitality; it has given
the world as much as it
has received from it.'
ISTVAN ÖRKÉNY
1978

Introduction

*A*t the turn of the century a traveller to Budapest neatly described the enigmatic quality of the city: 'If one is travelling from the east in the direction of western Europe, it is in Budapest that one experiences the breath of western civilisation. However, if one is travelling in the opposite direction, it is here that one first gets a taste of the east...' When the seven Magyar (Hungarian) tribes came over the Carpathians some 1,103 years ago, one group of them pitched their tents at this strategic point on the mighty River Danube. Although they were always to retain a proud memory of their Asian origins, they now began a new and settled existence in Europe.

In the Middle Ages the Royal Castle of Buda and its ancillary town grew wealthy under Magyar, Angevin and Luxembourg rulers. The subsequent 150-year-long Turkish occupation, and the Habsburg rule that followed it, then reduced Buda to provincial status. In the mid-19th century the hitherto insignificant town of Pest rapidly expanded into a great industrial metropolis. Until around 1860 half its inhabitants were German-speaking and there was also a large influx of Jews; most of the latter rapidly assimilated and became leading figures in the arts and in business. By 1900 Buda and Pest (united since 1873) had acquired the patina of mixed culture and frenetic capitalism which has now reappeared after 40 years of suspended animation under Communism.

Back to the future
As in other cities of the former Eastern

WHAT IT MEANS TO BE A MAGYAR

'Anyone who wants to understand Hungary,' writes the poet and journalist István Eörsi, 'needs to find the answer to one great secret: how is it that this country has survived at all? ... No nation is so experienced in defeat as the Hungarians.' This feeling of being the victims of history is recurrent in the Magyar psyche. On two occasions in the past – when the Tartars invaded in the 13th century and during the Turkish occupation – there was a real possibility of national extinction. In the 18th century the German philosopher, Johann Herder, predicted that the Magyar nation and culture would soon disappear, absorbed by their more numerous Slav and German neighbours. This prediction did not go unnoticed in Hungary, where men like Ferenc Kölcsey and Ferenc Kazinczy set about reviving the Hungarian language, and others promoted national aspirations. Yet it is language that most isolates Hungarians: for the writer Gyula Illyés, a Hungarian's native tongue is simultaneously the 'softest cradle and the most solid coffin'. Arthur Koestler summed up all these fears and contradictions in the Magyars' image of themselves when he wrote: 'To be Hungarian is a collective neurosis.'

Bloc, the gap between the haves and have-nots has widened rapidly since 1989.

New luxury hotels have been built and western car models stand gleaming in showrooms; but there are also the homeless, the beggars and the hard-pressed pensioners.

On the credit side Hungarians are natural entrepreneurs and much is being done to make the city hum again. With three fast elections behind them and the highest rate of foreign investment in the

❖

THOMAS COOK'S BUDAPEST

In 1885 Cook's were appointed official travel agents for a major agricultural exhibition staged by the Hungarian government. The first Thomas Cook office in Budapest was opened three years later, and Cook's were active in promoting the Millennial Exhibition (1896) and Budapest spas in the 1930s

❖

The coat of arms of the city of Budapest on Clark Ádám tér, a mosaic by Károly Lotz

former Eastern Bloc, Hungary approaches the Millennium with grounds for optimism, despite the shadow of poverty.

However, don't expect Hungarians to admit that things have improved. As the local saying goes: 'A pessimist is only a well-informed optimist'.

History

AD 106

The Roman garrison of *Aquincum* (situated in Óbuda) becomes the capital of Lower Pannonia.

5th century

According to legend, Attila the Hun ruled from the abandoned Roman amphitheatre in *Aquincum*. His younger brother, Bleda, is supposed to have given his name to a new city – 'Buda'.

896

Seven Magyar (Hungarian) tribes under Árpád cross the Carpathians and settle on the Danubian plains.

Late 10th century

The Magyar Prince Géza is converted to Christianity. His son Vajk is given Christian baptism as István (Stephen).

1000

Stephen is crowned King of Hungary on Christmas Day, with a crown sent by the Pope. Between 997 and 1038 King (later Saint) Stephen turned Hungary into a Christian feudal state.

1061

The first documentary reference to the town of Pest on the opposite side of the Danube to the Buda hill.

1241

Hungary is virtually destroyed by Tartar (Mongol) invaders. To rebuild the shattered country King Béla IV invites Germans and other foreigners to settle. The Castle of Buda is built (1247–65).

1301

The Hungarian Árpád line dies out. The House of Anjou succeeds, followed by Sigismund of Luxembourg in 1387, who vastly expands Buda castle.

1458–90

Under Matthias I (Corvinus) Buda reaches its architectural high point and is a great centre of Renaissance culture.

1526

Louis II of Hungary is disastrously defeated by the Turks at Mohács, Southern Hungary.

1541

Buda falls to the Turks. In the next 145 years they turn many Christian churches into mosques and exploit the spas to build baths.

1686

Armies led by Charles of Lorraine and

Statue of St Stephen on Castle Hill

Eugene of Savoy reconquer Buda.
Hungary falls under Habsburg rule.

1710–11

Buda and Pest are blockaded during the
War of Independence waged by Ferenc
Rákóczi II.

1740–80

German influence and economic
expansion increase under Maria
Theresa.

1795

A Jacobin revolt is defeated and its
ringleaders executed in Buda. The
popular Archduke Joseph (son of
Leopold II) becomes Palatine (viceroy)
of Hungary.

1820

Count István Széchenyi (1791–1860)
initiates the project for the first
permanent bridge linking Buda and Pest
(the Széchenyi Lánchíd – Chain Bridge).

1848

Hungary, under Lajos Kossuth, briefly
achieves independence from Habsburg
rule. The poet Sándor Petőfi distributes
his 'National Song' on the steps of the
National Museum.

1867

Emperor Franz Joseph and Ferenc Deák
(for the Hungarians) negotiate the
Ausgleich (Compromise). This brings
into being the Austro-Hungarian
Empire, a complicated system of dual
autonomy and joint rule.

1872–3

The towns of Buda, Óbuda and Pest are
united to form Budapest.

1896

The Millennial Celebrations mark 1,000
years of Hungary's existence. Pest's first
metro (leading to the Millennial
Monument on Heroes' Square) is built.

1918–19

Following defeat in World War I, the
Austro-Hungarian Empire collapses and
the Hungarian Republic is promulgated.
This is briefly succeeded by a
Communist Republic of Councils under
Béla Kun before Admiral Miklós Horthy
becomes Regent of Hungary.

1920

By the Treaty of Trianon Hungary loses
two-thirds of its territory. Three million
Hungarians are marooned in the
Empire's successor states.

1945

Soviet armies 'liberate' Budapest after an
immensely destructive nine-week siege.
In free elections the Smallholders' Party
wins 57 per cent of the vote. In 1948 the
Communists seize power.

1956

After several years of 'dictatorship of the
proletariat' under Mátyás Rákosi,
revolution breaks out in Budapest, only
to be suppressed by Soviet tanks. János
Kádár changes sides and forms a new
government with Soviet blessing.

1965–80s

The Kádár regime experiments with
'goulash' Communism and some
cautious market reforms.

1989

After Kádár is ousted in 1988, an interim
government of reform Communists
prepares the way for free elections, won
in 1990 by the right-of-centre Hungarian
Democratic Forum led by József Antall.
An opposition Free Democrat is elected
Mayor of Budapest.

1990–4

Much industry is privatised in market
reforms, but living standards fall.

1994

In May the Socialists and Free
Democrats win the elections.

1998

The right-of-centre Hungarian Civic
Party under Viktor Orbán forms a
government with the Smallholders' Party.

1956 AND ALL THAT

The heroism of the Hungarian revolution of 1956 has passed into history – a brave battle against appalling odds. For a few brief days of euphoria it looked as if it might succeed, and the Stalinist tyranny seemed on the brink of extinction.

Pressure for change came first from the so-called 'Petőfi Circle', named after Hungary's national poet and freedom fighter. Then student demonstrations attracted thousands of supporters. Finally factory workers became the driving force of the revolution. Much of the Hungarian army, led by Pál Maléter, also fought for freedom.

Timetable of a Revolution
6 October 1956
200,000 people attend the reburial of László Rajk, the Interior Minister executed after a show-trial by the Rákosi regime.
23 October
In solidarity with the Polish opposition, students lead a march to the statue of the Polish general and Hungarian freedom fighter, József Bem. At 6pm Imre Nagy, previously expelled from the Party for his espousal of more humane government as prime minister in 1953, speaks to vast crowds before the Parliament.

At 11pm students besiege the radio and the ÁVH (Security Service) open fire on them.
24 October
Imre Nagy becomes prime minister. Soviet tanks move on Budapest.
31 October
A truce is arranged and Soviet tanks withdraw.
1 November
Nagy announces that Hungary is to leave the Warsaw Pact.
3 November
Pál Maléter, negotiating with the Soviet Army under guarantee of safe-conduct, is arrested.
4 November
Soviet Army reinvades. János Kádár announces the formation of his puppet government. Nagy flees to the Yugoslav Embassy.

22 November
Nagy leaves the Yugoslav Embassy with a promise of safe-conduct and is arrested.
16 June 1958
Nagy and Maléter are executed.

Aftermath of a Revolution
While the borders remained open, 200,000 people fled the country. There were an estimated

Scenes from the 1956 Revolution

'If my life is necessary to prove that not all Communists are enemies of the people, then I willingly give it up.' IMRE NAGY, reportedly his last words in 1958.

2,000 revenge executions; thousands more were imprisoned.

16 June 1989

Some 250,000 people attended a ceremony on Heroes' Square to honour Imre Nagy and Pál Maléter, whose remains were reburied.

6 July 1989

On the day the Supreme Court declared Nagy innocent of the charges on which he was convicted and executed, János Kádár died.

Politics

*I*n 1989 the satellite regimes of Soviet Russia buckled one by one under the combined pressure of failing economies and Mikhail Gorbachev's policy of *glasnost* (openness). The smoothest transition from totalitarianism to democracy came about in Hungary, chiefly because the last Communist government accepted the inevitable gracefully.

The end of Communism

During János Kádár's long rule (1956–88), the oppressive paraphernalia of Stalinism had been softened and a small private sector allowed to develop. This had led to Hungary being regarded as 'the happiest barracks in the Socialist camp'. But in the '80s the country suffered from rising inflation and an alarming increase in foreign debt. The ageing Kádár compounded his economic mismanagement by the decision to go ahead with an ecologically catastrophic dam at Nagymáros on the Danube, part of a joint energy project with the Slovaks.

At the May 1988 Party Congress reformers and technocrats joined forces to oust Kádár from the leadership. By July 1989 four of them, under the impressive leadership of the youthful Miklós Németh, were in control of the government. By October the Communists had reconstituted themselves as the Socialist Party, the 'iron curtain' on the Austrian border had been dismantled and free elections announced for the following year. In November, on the 33rd anniversary of the 1956 revolution (see pages 10–11), the Republic of Hungary was proclaimed.

The elections of 1990

Two parties dominated the second round of voting (25 March): the populist and conservative Hungarian Democratic Forum and the intellectual metropolitan Alliance of Free Democrats, with Democratic Forum emerging a clear winner. A worrying sign was the low turn-out, which seemed to indicate that much of the electorate expected very little to be achieved by any political grouping. The government subsequently formed by József Antall was a coalition that included the revived Smallholders' Party (winners of the last free elections in 1945, but now a sentimental relic) and the Christian Democrats. A distinguished Free Democrat and former Communist victim, Árpád Göncz, was elected president by Parliament.

The Antall Government

In facing the severe economic and political problems inherited from Communism, the Antall government looked increasingly beleaguered. Its image was also tarnished by the right-wing of the Democratic Forum, led by the writer István Csurka, indulging in anti-Semitic rhetoric and demanding witch-hunts against former Communists.

Until his death in December 1993, Antall ploughed on with his strategy of gradual adjustment to the free market economy. But while fiscal retrenchment and conscientious debt servicing have preserved Hungary's credit rating on the financial markets, inflation at over 20 per cent, high unemployment and social hardship produced a Socialist victory in the 1994 elections.

Hungary at the crossroads

As the 1990s advance, there are many negative factors in Hungarian life. The economy has been buffeted by the world recession and the reluctance of the European Union to admit competitively priced Hungarian products. Society has been strained by the contrast between the poverty of many and the wealth of a few. The public frequently turns in disgust from politicians seemingly more interested in the spoils of power than in the enlightened use of it.

Yet there are also grounds for optimism. Growth has recommenced and the country has attracted the most foreign investment of the former Eastern Bloc countries. The incoming government of 1998 is youthful and pragmatic, although hampered by an arch-conservative coalition partner. Above all Hungarians are entrepreneurial and resourceful as a nation: if the opportunities arise, they will be quick to seize them.

Freedom Monument on Gellért-hegy

Geography

*B*udapest lies 47 degrees 23 minutes north and 19 degrees 9 minutes east, on either side of the River Danube (Duna). Within the river's 28km passage through the city, the width of the channel varies between 1km and 230m.

The mighty waterway has shaped the character of the city. For the Romans it was a defensive barrier – they built their garrison and administrative capital at *Aquincum* on the western bank. The Magyar kings shifted the focus to the natural citadel of Buda Hill, while Pest was the gateway to the east, a town of travellers and traders, later the dynamic centre of business and industry.

In the landscape, too, the characteristics of the two cities reflect different aspects of Hungary: from the flattish terrain of Pest, the Alföld (Great Hungarian Plain) stretches to the east and south; on the west bank the gentle hills of Buda (the highest is the 529m János-hegy) point the way to the rolling landscapes of Transdanubia.

Economy

Hungary has nearly completed a painful restructuring of its economy following the collapse of Communism and the disappearance of traditional markets in the Eastern Bloc. Inflation is still too high at around 15% and there is still a current account deficit of around $2 billion. But economic recovery is now palpable, with a growth rate of 4.4%, achieved by restructuring and substantial reorientation of exports away from Russia, although Hungary was still hit by the 1998 economic crisis in Russia. The service sector has been revitalised thanks to substantial foreign investment. Money from abroad is also helping other industries, such as breweries and automobile factories.

Environment

Like other former Eastern Bloc cities Budapest suffers from a decaying infrastructure and serious pollution. In 1992 academics and lawyers formed an Environmental Management and Law

Harvesting near Pécs, southern Hungary

GOODBYE TRABI!

An elegiac piece in the press of 1991 lamented the passing of East German imports – the 'Trabi' (Trabant), which provided an experience 'like riding a four-wheel moped in a raincoat'; the Practica 35mm SLR, 'a good workhorse camera designed for planets without gravity'; and 'nifty kitchen wares made of slag-iron'.

Pollution has taken a heavy toll on many of Pest's façades

Association in an attempt to push environmental concerns to the top of the political agenda.

Another initiative, by the mayor of Budapest, offered owners of smoke-belching two-stroke Trabants free passes for public transport and low-interest loans if they give up their cars. A start has also been made on cleaning up energy production: the Kelenföld Power Station, which supplies 36,000 homes, has been rebuilt for gas turbine production of electricity, using waste gases to heat the boilers at a cost of 100 million dollars. The reduction in sulphur dioxide was about 80 per cent, in nitrogen oxide 40 per cent.

Budapest's water supply is endangered by the Slovak government's decision to persist with the Gabcikovo hydroelectric dam on the Danube, a legacy of totalitarian planning. Hungary pulled out of the project in 1992, refusing to complete the complementary dam at Nagymáros on Hungarian territory. The fertile agricultural area of Szigetköz in western Hungary is already badly affected. The reduction of emissions and the cleaning of public buildings, however, have given Budapest a new face.

Investment in infrastructure will take longer, but the telephone system (formerly chaotic) has been modernised and an urgently needed ring road to stop lorries thundering through built-up areas was completed in 1994.

'The backbone of Hungary will be the small and middle-sized entrepreneurs.'
PETER ZWACK, after regaining control of his family firm making the aperitif *Unicum*, expropriated by the Communists.

People and Culture

*T*he numerous warm, healing springs of the Budapest area attracted settlers from earliest times, the first of them occupying the limestone caves formed by spa waters on the Danube's west bank. Eventually these spas were to become a significant source of wealth for the inhabitants (see pages 34–5). The Danube itself was crucial to the development of Hungary, bringing trade and valuable immigrants, as well as less welcome invaders and floods.

The historic name of the Hungarian people is 'Magyars', 'Hungary' being 'Magyarország'. Now much diluted, the Magyars are descended from the Ugrian branch of the Finno-Ugric people who once populated the land between the Urals and the River Ob. While their northern cousins, the Finns and Estonians, are descendants of the group that migrated north and west around 2000BC, the Magyars were influenced by Turkic and other cultures around the Caucasus before crossing into the Carpathian Basin in AD896.

City population

Buda and Pest have had a mixed population, including foreign craftsmen and merchants, since early times. Large numbers of Germans were settled by Maria Theresa in order to rebuild the country after 150 years of Turkish

devastation: then in the 19th century thousands of Jews migrated to Hungary from Moravia and Galicia, the majority settling in Pest.

Today the population of Budapest is just over two million, one in five of the Hungarians living within Hungary (some five million live beyond the borders, most of them as minorities in neighbouring countries).

Religion

Hungary has been Christian since the 11th century, when King Stephen forcibly converted the population. Although Orthodoxy had a toehold of influence through royal marriages, the country was firmly Catholic until the Reformation, but 90 per cent of Hungarians had become Protestant by the late 16th century. Habsburg rule and its attendant Counter-Reformation sought to reverse this situation, but Protestantism hung on in the east and on the Great Plain. Today Hungary is 57 per cent Catholic and 30 per cent Protestant.

A European culture

Hungary's artistic legacy substantially reflects the country's attachment to the traditions of Western European culture, and the further back we look, the more

The lush interior of Miklós Ybl's opera house

Modern statue of Franz Liszt by László Martou on the square named after him

apparent this becomes. From the establishment of the feudal state under King Stephen (997–1038) until the Turkish invasions in the 16th century, Hungary was part of the supra-national European Christian culture. Artists and craftsmen came from the Low Countries, Germany and Italy to work for the Hungarian kings of the late Árpád, Anjou and Luxembourg dynasties. The Cistercian, Benedictine and Premonstratensian orders built churches in the pan-European Romanesque and Gothic styles: fine examples have survived at Ják in Western Hungary and Bélapátfalva in the east.

The palaces of Buda and Visegrád (see pages 38/127) reached the summit of splendour under King Matthias Corvinus (1458–90), who invited the best Italian craftsmen to work there. His Renaissance court was a glittering centre of the arts and humanist scholarship. Half a century later Hungary was dismembered in the Turkish wars; Transylvania retained its political and cultural autonomy under the leadership of Protestant princes, but the rest of the territory was carved up between the Turks and the Habsburgs.

The rise of national culture

The expulsion of the Turks at the end of the 17th century brought with it the Counter-Reformation and Habsburg dominance. The baroque town of Buda and baroque churches in Pest date to this period. National resistance to the Austrian oppressors was conducted through warfare in the 18th century, but increasingly found expression through culture after Emperor Joseph II (1780–90) tried to Germanise his Hungarian subjects. The epics of Mihály Vörösmarty (1800–55) revived consciousness of Magyar history and the poet Sándor Petőfi became a hero of the 1848 war of independence against the Habsburgs. The early 19th-century architecture of Pest, while reflecting the Central European taste for neo-classicism, was created by Hungarian masters such as Mihály Pollack and József Hild. Later in the 19th century Miklós Ybl built many of the great neo-Renaissance palaces on the graceful boulevards of the expanding city.

Back to the roots

In the late 19th century, we encounter a different kind of Hungarian self-perception, one that reconciles semi-mythical eastern roots with western civilisation. The national revival in literature began with the proclamation by Ferenc Kölcsey (author of the Hungarian national anthem) that poetry must be sought 'in the songs of the common people', while in the late 19th century architects and artists began to create in a consciously Hungarian manner. Ödön Lechner (see pages 58–9) was one such architect, and Károly Kós (see page 140), in the early years of the 20th century, drew inspiration from Transylvanian vernacular forms and the English arts and crafts movement. The latter also influenced the members of the Gödöllő artists' colony, founded in 1902 near Budapest, whose work exploited Hungarian folk motifs. In the fine arts the *plein air* school of Nagybánya produced distinctively Hungarian landscape painting, while the idiosyncratic work of Tivadar Csontváry Kosztka embodied a mystical sense of Hungarian identity.

In music Franz Liszt was the first to popularise Hungarian themes. He also founded the Budapest Music Academy, which was to nurture innumerable great talents. In 1905 Béla Bartók and Zoltán Kodály began their great work of systematically collecting Hungarian folk music from all over the country and this was to influence their own music.

Statue of Béla Bartók in the garden of his house

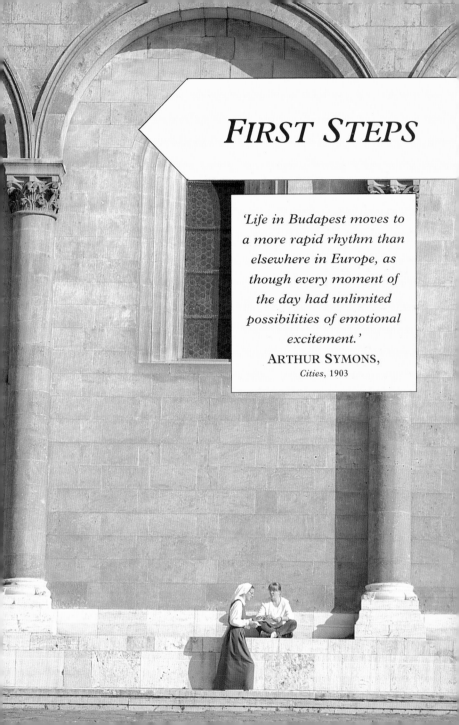

FIRST STEPS

'Life in Budapest moves to a more rapid rhythm than elsewhere in Europe, as though every moment of the day had unlimited possibilities of emotional excitement.'
ARTHUR SYMONS,
Cities, 1903

First Steps

*T*he outskirts of Budapest are little different from those of other cities of the former Eastern Bloc: decaying factories ring the Pest side and blocks of pre-fabricated 'panel housing' disfigure the skyline. Luckily, Budapest is still a modest-sized city by contemporary European standards and the centre is quickly reached from the airport.

The historic cores of Pest and Buda hug opposite banks of the Danube. You can gain an overall impression of them by taking one of the trams that run along either side of the river (from Jászai Mari tér or Batthyány tér); or you could climb to the Halászbástya (Fishermen's Bastion) on Castle Hill for a bird's-eye view of Pest.

Pest is a bustling, lively town with towering 19th-century blocks and great boulevards. At first it is easy to get lost in the urban density of the Belváros (Inner

City); but a few minutes' walk in any direction brings you to a major landmark, square or avenue. By contrast, residential Buda is on a smaller scale and more private, while Castle Hill is an historical tableau.

In his *Budapest Walks* of 1916, city chronicler Gyula Krúdy wrote: 'This city smells of violets in the spring, as do the ladies along the promenade above the river on the Pest side. In the fall it is Buda that suggests the tone: the odd thud of chestnuts dropping on the castle walk, fragments of the music of a military band wafting over the forlorn silence: autumn and Buda were born of the same mother.' Today, though a Transylvanian fiddler may have replaced the military band and the ladies on the promenade in front of the luxury hotels are redolent of high fashion names like Gucci or Benetton rather than smelling of violets, nostalgia is in: Budapest is selling old style to a new clientele.

When to go
Central Europe's continental climate is extremely hot in summer, raw and cold in winter. The nicest times to visit are between April and the end of June and, especially, between September and the end of October. The long Indian summer provides ideal weather for excursions (see pages 124–34). If you must visit in high

Ferihegy airport

summer, strategies for keeping cool include heading for the spas (see pages 32–3) during the heat of the day and lodging in the Buda Hills rather than down in the stifling city. An August bonus is the spectacular fireworks display from Gellért-hegy (Gellért Hill) on the 20th, St Stephen's Day. This usually marks the beginning of the end of the *canicula* – as Hungarians call the broiling mid-summer season. The Budapest Arts Weeks kick off on the anniversary of Béla Bartók's birth (25 September); other events include a wine festival and an international dog show in May.

Arriving
Direct flights from European capitals and America arrive at Ferihegy, Budapest's international airport, 16km to the east of the city centre. Budapest has several daily rail connections to Vienna, trains arriving and leaving from the Déli pályaudvar (Southern Railway Station) or the Keleti pályaudvar (Eastern Railway Station) according to the time of day. Both have direct metro connections to the centre, as does the Nyugati pályaudvar (Western Railway Station), which serves Prague. From April to September a hydrofoil runs twice daily on the Danube between Vienna and Budapest, taking four and a half hours.

The majority of travellers by car arrive via Vienna, which is well served by the German/Austrian Autobahn network. A new motorway now runs from Vienna to the Hungarian border at Nickelsdorf/Hegyeshalom and on (100km) to Budapest, the Hungarian section being a toll road. An Autobahn sticker must also be purchased for the Austrian section.

The Western Railway Station

'Trabants' can still be seen on the streets

advisable to buy an up-to-date street plan on arrival – as late as 1993 some street names were still being changed, although in some cases the old name (with a red line through it) has been left beside the new. It is worth buying the modestly priced three-day excursion ticket (*Háromnapos túristajegy*), valid on all forms of city transport and on sale at larger metro stations and tobacconists.

The metro has three lines, colour coded blue, red and yellow and all meeting at the central junction on Deák Ferenc tér. The blue line runs across Pest, the red one crosses the Danube to south Buda and the yellow follows the radial Andrássy út through the centre of Pest. Trolley buses run only on the Pest side. Trams run along either side of the Danube, along the Pest boulevards and on main arteries elsewhere. There is also an excellent bus service, but be aware that you need to press the button over the door if you wish to get off. The HÉV suburban railway is useful for excursions (to Szentendre from Batthyány tér or Ráckeve from Kőzvágóhíd – see pages 132 and 138). Precise transport details are given in the Practical Guide, page 188.

Other means of transport in Budapest are principally for sightseeing. The boats criss-crossing the Danube afford views of the Országház (Parliament) and Buda Castle from the river; a cable car (Sikló) runs up to Castle Hill from Clark Ádám tér; a chairlift takes you from Zugliget to János-hegy in the Buda Hills; a cogwheel railway (Fogaskerekű) runs from Városmajor on the Buda side up to Széchenyi-hegy (Széchenyi Hill); the Children's Railway (see page 154) runs

Getting around

Getting around in Budapest is no great problem for the visitor, although unpronounceable names may cause difficulties at first. The areas of interest to visitors are relatively small and compact, and are well served by metro, trams, trolley buses and buses. It is

Chain Bridge (Széchenyi lánchíd)

Fiakers can be used for painless sightseeing on Castle Hill

through the Buda woods.

Taxis are cheap by western standards. There are rather too many rogues – stick to the well-established companies: Budataxi, City Taxi and Fötaxi (which has the best reputation).

Manners and mores

Hungarians do not expect foreigners to master their language, but it is best to learn greetings, which are always offered on entering or leaving a shop or in addressing strangers. These are: *jó reggelt kívánok* (good morning), *jó napot kívánok* (good day – from about 10am), *jó estét kívánok* (good evening) and *jó éjszakát kívánok* (goodnight). *Viszontlátásra* is goodbye (see **Language** in the **Practical Guide**). Silence or a nod could be taken as rudeness.

When you introduce yourself or are introduced always shake hands and say your complete name. Your interlocutor will do likewise, but remember Hungarian names are in reverse order,

whether written or spoken. Thus Englishman John Smith meets Hungarian Kovács János (Smith John).

Hungarians are extremely hospitable and proud housewives will probably press on you more food than you want. Trying to foot the bill in a restaurant is usually a struggle – accept *force majeure* with a good grace unless there are compelling reasons for not doing so. If you are invited to somebody's home, flowers for the hostess and perhaps wine for the host are usual. You may be asked to remove your shoes and put on house slippers – simply to protect the invariably spotless home! When it comes to the meal, never drink before your host has raised his glass and wished everyone good health.

Feminists will note that male chauvinism is alive and well, often masquerading as old-style gallantry. Yet quite battle-hardened ladies have been known to melt just a little when greeted with '*kezét csókolom*' (I kiss your hand).

BUDAPEST

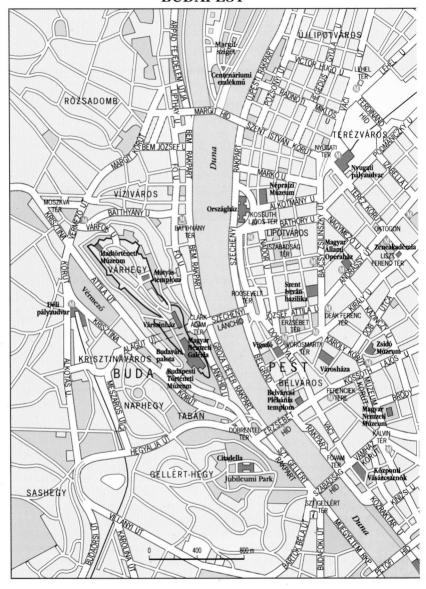

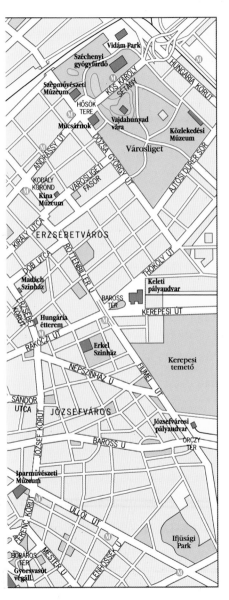

Areas of Budapest

Administration

For administrative purposes Budapest is divided into 22 districts, of which about 10 will be of interest to the visitor. The others are primarily residential or industrial. District numbers are required for post codes, but otherwise people stick to names sanctioned by custom and use.

Districts of Buda

The Buda side of the Danube is dominated by Várhegy (Castle Hill), below which is the Víziváros (Water Town) stretching as far as Moszkva tér behind the hill's northern tip. To the northwest is Rózsadomb (the Hill of Roses), where the most sought-after villas are to be found. Further north is Óbuda and to the south, beyond the Gellért-hegy (Gellért Hill), is the rather bleak suburb of Kelenföld; beyond that is an area half developed for the World Exhibition which was abandoned.

Districts of Pest

Central Pest is divided by two boulevards, unofficially known as Kiskörút (Little Ringroad, running laterally from Margit híd to Szabadság híd) and Nagykörút (Greater Ringroad, running in a wider arc from Margit híd to Petőfi híd). The fifth district is enclosed by the Little Ringroad and contains the major sights, although some lie between the two boulevards.

Further east are the City Woodland Park (Városliget), the sports stadia of Istvánmező and the Kerepesi temető (Kerepesi Cemetery – see page 50).

Background to Buda

*T*he Gellért Hill and the small plateau of the Buda Castle with its adjacent town rise on the west bank of the Danube. Between the plateau and the river is a narrow strip of land settled since the Middle Ages and known as Víziváros (Water Town). To the north is Óbuda (Old Buda – see page 30).

Gellért-hegy (Gellért Hill)

This dolomite rock (235m) was the earliest inhabited part of Budapest. In prehistoric times cave-dwellers took advantage of the hot springs bursting through a geological fault – springs that still supply the Gellért spa today. In Roman times the surviving Celts lived in this area, some 2km from the military and civil settlements of *Aquincum* to the north. Nowadays the hill is an agreeable park (see page 48) with footpaths winding up to the Freedom Monument and Citadella on the summit. The grotto

chapel (just above the Gellért Hotel) has recently been reconsecrated, after being walled up by the Communists (who, incidentally, located their command bunker, for use in the event of Armageddon, in the bowels of the Gellért rock).

Várhegy (Castle Hill)

The town and fortress of Buda only achieved real significance in the second half of the 10th century. Of the four ancient royal and religious centres in Hungary – Székesfehérvár, Esztergom (see page 126), Veszprém and Buda – the last to develop was Buda. An economic boom in the 11th and 12th centuries led to expansion of Buda, Óbuda and Pest, and an increase in religious foundations. The Tartar invasion of 1241 devastated the whole region, but thereafter King Béla IV, known as the refounder of the nation, encouraged settlers from abroad and built the first fortress on Buda Hill.

The rise of Buda

The basic layout of the town of Buda, which has endured until today, dates from the last third of the 13th century, when the two-storeyed Gothic houses for wealthy burghers were built. Buda had two communities: the Germans, whose Church of Our Lady (later the Matthias Church) stood to the south; and the Hungarians, whose Church of Mary

Poet Attila József sculpted in brooding pose

The Parliament (Országház) as seen from Buda

Magdalene was at the northern end.

The first Anjou king, Charles Robert (1308–42), chose to build his great palace upstream of Buda at Visegrád (see page 127), and it was not until 1347 that Louis I ('the Great') moved his court to Buda and major expansion of the Royal Palace began. Sigismund of Luxembourg (1387–1437) built a lavish new palace in the 15th century and invited masters from Paris, Stuttgart and Augsburg to decorate it. The apotheosis was reached under Matthias Corvinus (1458–90), whose Italian masons and craftsmen created the most glittering royal court in contemporary Europe.

Decline and restoration

After the Turkish conquest of 1541 churches were vandalised and turned into mosques; Buda slowly decayed until its liberation by Habsburg troops in 1686, though the reconquest itself left most of the town in ruins. A small baroque Buda subsequently grew up, together with a very plain and functional baroque palace, erected under Maria Theresa.

In the late 18th and early 19th centuries the officials of the Palatine lived in Buda and the Diet met there (for the last time in 1807). While Pest expanded rapidly, Buda stagnated, although areas bordering on Castle Hill such as Krisztinaváros and Rózsadomb became desirable residential areas. The last rebuilding of the Royal Palace took place after the 1867 Ausgleich (Compromise) with the Habsburgs, that created the Austro-Hungarian Empire. Subsequently Buda was destroyed by the Russian siege at the end of World War II and rebuilt in the 1950s and '60s as a showcase of historic restoration.

Background to Pest

*T*he origins of Pest lie in the Roman period, when a small fortress to protect the ferry crossing at the narrows was built at what is now the Pest end of the Erzsébet híd (Elizabeth Bridge). In the late 10th century traders settled near the ferry to exploit the Danubian ship traffic.

In the 11th century a burial chapel for St Gellért was erected, the first sanctuary on the site of the Belvárosi plébániatemplom (Inner City Parish Church – see page 44). The unfortunate missionary had in fact been about to cross from the Buda side when he was intercepted and drowned in the river by supporters of the pagan faction (1046). Shortly afterwards (1061) the first documentary mention of the town of Pest appears.

Medieval and baroque Pest

In the 11th and 12th centuries Pest expanded to become a substantial and wealthy trading town, with a royal residence, a Dominican cloister and a parish church. After the Tartar invasion of 1241, King Béla IV renewed its privileges of a Royal Free Town, but many of its mainly German inhabitants moved to the comparative safety of Buda. In the 14th century it boomed again under the Anjou dynasty, when the parish church was enlarged and altered to the form of a *Hallenkirche* (hall church).

After the Turkish occupation (1541–1686), building began again in Pest; a hospital for war veterans was built

Strolling on the bastions of Castle Hill

by Italian architects in 1716, together with several baroque convents and churches (for example those of the Servites, the Franciscans and the Hungarian order of Paulites). Of the baroque palaces built by aristocrats, few traces remain; Andras Mayerhoffer's Péterffy Palace (1755) in Pesti Barnabás utca (now the Százéves restaurant) is a rare example.

Expansion

Pest came into its own in the 19th century. In 1805 János Hild presented his plans to improve the city to the Embellishment Commission supported by the Palatine. The proposed parks and public buildings were to be financed by selling building plots and by the revenues of customs and local taxes. The inner city (Belváros) thereafter became a largely residential area with churches and schools. Neighbouring Lipótváros (Leopold's Town) was the business centre, increasingly also the domain of wealthy assimilated Jews. Neo-classical buildings – the Magyar Nemzeti Múzeum (National Museum), the Calvinist and Lutheran Churches – gave the city its monumental character up to the revolution against the Habsburgs of 1848, when many neo-classical dwellings were destroyed.

In the second half of the 19th century Pest became the hub of a rapidly expanding and industrialising capital. Whereas in 1850 the populations of Buda and Pest were roughly equal, by 1900 only one in six Budapestians lived in Buda. The great boulevards crossed by the radial of Andrássy út were now built, as were three new bridges. Miklós Ybl planted magnificent neo-Renaissance palaces along the streets and designed a graceful opera house (1884). Theatres, museums and hotels, many on a grand scale, enriched the cityscape of Pest. The

The church of Krisztínaváros from Castle Hill

monumental Szent István bazilika (St Stephen's Basilica) was begun in 1851 and the even more monumental Országház (Parliament) was completed just after the turn of the century. The Millennial Celebrations of 1896 put the seal on all this dynamism and self-confidence, while the idiosyncratic buildings of Ödön Lechner and his school gave expression to the Magyar soul in architecture.

In the 20th century Pest has begun to sprawl, pushing out subtopian tentacles; but at its heart is still the bustle and business of that dynamic 19th-century city, now reawakening to capitalistic enterprise, artistic creativity and gourmet refinement.

The Ancient Town of Óbuda

*T*he Roman province of Pannonia was created in the first century BC and divided by Trajan into Upper and Lower Pannonia around AD 106. *Aquincum* (see pages 76–7) was the civil capital of Lower Pannonia. Close to it was the military *castrum* (at the Óbuda end of Árpád híd/Árpád Bridge) and its associated domestic buildings known as *canabae*.

Two of the chiefs of the seven Magyar tribes (Kende and Kurszán) took up residence in Óbuda, and the first church – a burial chapel built over the grave of the paramount chief, Árpád – was raised in Óbuda at the end of the 10th or the beginning of the 11th century.

In the Middle Ages the town

increased in wealth and importance, particularly under Béla III, who entertained Frederick Barbarossa here in 1189. A Cistercian cloister was built, and other religious orders followed in the 14th century, when the widowed queen of King Charles Robert of Anjou moved her palace to the town. Under Sigismund of Luxembourg Óbuda even boasted a university (founded in 1389, the first in Hungary).

Like Buda and Pest, the town suffered under the Turkish occupation, but in the 18th century the Habsburgs bestowed the Óbuda lands on the Zichy family. They built their great mansion close to Fő tér (see page 111), and encouraged Jews to settle, thus boosting the area's economy. Crafts and trade received further stimulation in the 19th century when Count Széchenyi founded the shipyard on Óbuda Island and the Goldberger textile factory began operations (both still exist).

Sadly Óbuda has suffered from the ravages of time and Communism. The once picturesque provincial town is now a concrete jungle with a few isolated pockets of baroque charm and elegance. A visit to these relics (and the delightful local museum at Kiscelli) will give a hint of past glories.

Fő tér in Óbuda

WHAT TO SEE

'I had heard Budapest described as the most beautiful city in Europe.
It is strange and dramatic, to be sure, but there is something rather barbaric about it. It wants to belong to the West, but one remembers the Mongolians and the Turks.'

EDMUND WILSON
Notes from a European Diary (Europe without Baedeker), 1963–4

Baths of Buda and Pest

Of Budapest's many public baths, the four described here all have good facilities, interesting historical features and architectural charm.

GELLÉRT GYÓGYFÜRDŐ
(Gellért Spa)

The Buda spa most popular with visitors is where the earliest inhabitants exploited the mineral springs of the Gellért Hill; later a local hermit worked miracles with the water; and later still the poor of Buda bathed here (and watered their horses) during the Turkish occupation.

The present establishment goes back to a decision of the City Council in 1901 to purchase the land and exploit the springs, whose outlet had been covered over when the Szabadság híd (Freedom Bridge) was built in 1896. Plans for a hotel and spa were finally approved in 1909. By the summer of 1914 only the walls had been built, but despite the outbreak of war the building was completed, and opened in 1918.

The architecture is in an agreeably over-the-top version of Jugendstil. The main indoor pool (with jets of bubbles pumped from the floor for 10 minutes each hour) presents a fantasia of mosaics, columns and gushing gargoyles. The entrance hall recalls the grandiosity of the Caracalla Baths in Rome, while frivolity is catered for in the 'wave-bath' in the ornamental terraced gardens at the rear. *Kelenhegyi út 2–4. Tel: 166–6166. Open: October to May, Monday to Friday 6am–7pm, Saturday and Sunday 6am–4pm; May to September, Monday to Friday 6am–7pm, Saturday and Sunday pool 6am–7pm, spa 6am–5pm. Trams 47, 49 (from Pest), 18, 19 (Buda side).*

KIRÁLY GYÓGYFÜRDŐ (King Spa)

The bath, built by Pasha Mustapha Sokollu, was completed in 1578. There was no thermal spring near by, so water was piped from the Lukács area (see below). The ground-plan of the bath is a rectangle, on which has been built an octagonal basin over-arched by a cupola studded with tiny hexagonal light-wells.

The bath had several owners after the reconquest of 1686, the last (1796) being a certain Ferenc König (Király in

Széchenyi Spa

The wave bath of Buda's most popular spa, the Gellért

Hungarian), from whom it takes its name. The charming neo-classical wing was added in 1826.

Fő utca 84. Tel: 202–3688. Open for women: Tuesday and Thursday 6.30am–6pm, Saturday 6.30am–1pm. For men: Monday, Wednesday and Friday 6.30am–6pm. Admission charge. Metro to Batthyány tér.

LUKÁCS GYÓGY-ÉS STRANDFÜRDŐ (St Luke Spa)

Under the Turks the spring here was used to drive a gunpowder mill, although a hospital spa named after St Luke had occupied the site of the present baths in the Middle Ages. Baths were once more in operation here by the 1850s, enlarged in 1863 and again in 1884 when the powder mill was finally discontinued.

Lukács is an oasis of calm and charm with its huge courtyard lying in the shade of ancient plane-trees. The clientele is intellectual and professional, gossip being as important an activity here as bathing.

Frankel Leó út 25–29. Tel: 326–1695. Open (pool): Monday to Saturday 6am–8pm, Sunday 6am–7pm. Thermal pool 6.30am–8pm. Men on Tuesday, Thursday, Saturday and Sunday; women on Monday Wednesday and Friday. Admission charge. Tram 17 (Buda side).

SZÉCHENYI GYÓGYFÜRDŐ (Széchenyi Spa)

The most impressive spa on the Pest side, named after Count István Széchenyi, opened in 1913 (enlarged 1927). It is a rambling neo-baroque establishment supplied by a thermal spring discovered in 1876. The water rises from a depth of 1,256m at a temperature of 70°C.

Állatkerti körút 11 (in Városliget). Tel: 121–0310. Open: Monday to Friday 6am–7pm, Saturday and Sunday 6am–1pm. Admission charge. Metro to Széchenyi Fürdő.

SPA CITY

In the prehistory of Buda hundreds of spring-fed streams trickled off the hills into a riparian swamp, and thence into the Danube. When the Celtic Eravisci arrived, they occupied the Gellért Hill and probably other parts of the west bank. The Romans took over the picturesque name the Celts had given to their settlement – Ak-Ink, meaning 'Abundant Waters' – and Latinised it to *Aquincum.*

There is still a Római fürdő (Roman bath) near the ruins of *Aquincum,* one of three fed by a source at nearby Csillaghegy. It seems that the Magyars too exploited the waters, for the newcomers divided Buda into areas known as Felsőhévíz (Upper Thermal Waters) and Alsóhévíz (Lower Thermal Waters). In the Middle Ages at least two hospitals based on spas were founded (at today's Gellért and Lukács baths) by the Knights Hospitallers of St John. For the Turks bathing had a ritual significance; between 1541 and 1686 numerous Turkish baths were built, today almost the sole architectural and cultural legacy of Ottoman rule.

The spas of Buda and Pest evoke memories of a leisured age

facilities. The water temperature varies between 24° and 78°C. Many of the springs are sulphurous or slightly radioactive: they are used to treat rheumatism, circulation disorders and gynaecological complaints.

Budapest was officially designated a spa city in 1934 by the International Spa Congress (which subsequently moved its headquarters to the city). It certainly deserves the title, for there are 123 springs in Buda, Óbuda and Pest, spouting an estimated 70 million litres of water daily and supplying 47 baths, of which 12 have extensive medical

Budapest baths have something for everybody: there are open-air and sports pools, artificial wave baths and bubble baths, medicinal and mud baths, warm, cool and Turkish baths. All those pounds put on from consumption of heavy Magyar dishes can (theoretically) be lost again in the city's 'abundant waters'.

Bridges

*I*n 1870, when Gusztáv Zsigmondy was carrying out a regulation of the Danube, he discovered, just north of today's Árpád Bridge, the sunken piles of a wooden Roman bridge. This was the first and last Budapest bridge until the 19th century (see pages 82–3).

Although Sigismund of Luxembourg and Matthias Corvinus seem to have planned stone bridges in the 15th century, nothing came of their projects. A pontoon was in operation by the beginning of the 16th century; Turkish engineers subsequently built a more sophisticated 70-drum version roughly where the Elizabeth Bridge is now. After the reconquest an ingenious so-called 'flying bridge' was put into operation by enterprising Viennese. It consisted of a catamaran attached to the banks by long ropes resting on barges. By manipulating the rudder, the boat could be made to swing from shore to shore, using the force of the current. It was in use until 1790, by which time an elegant 'swaying promenade' with 43 pontoons had been built. Opened at dawn and midday to let through river traffic, it had to be dismantled in winter because of ice-floes. The municipal authorities would bed the safe paths across the ice with straw, charging users double the pontoon toll (though nobles, soldiers and students went free). During a big freeze, fairs and balls would be held on the river. The last ball (in 1883) ended in tragedy when the ice suddenly gave way, tipping the dance floor into the glacial waters. Forty people drowned.

Freedom Bridge (formerly Franz Joseph Bridge)

Building and naming bridges

Since the first of Budapest's bridges in modern times was completed in 1848, seven have been built within the city boundaries. Two more are planned to relieve traffic congestion in the centre. The vicissitudes of history are reflected in the various name changes: today's 'Liberty Bridge' was planned as 'Customs House Square Bridge', but inaugurated by the Emperor himself as 'Franz Joseph Bridge'. The 'Chain Bridge' later became 'Széchenyi Chain Bridge' in honour of its originator, while 'Petőfi Bridge' to the south for a while bore the name of the inter-war regent, Miklós Horthy.

The Árpád Bridge to the north was officially 'Stalin Bridge' in the 1950s, and reverted to its original name after the 1956 revolution. All Budapest bridges had to be rebuilt after the war, having been blown up by the retreating Germans.

Building the Elizabeth Bridge greatly altered the landscape on the Pest side

ERZSÉBET HÍD (Elizabeth Bridge)

The 290m suspension bridge was built between 1897 and 1903 and reconstructed to a modern design after World War I. Its structure weighs just over 1,000 tonnes, but carries 29 90-tonne components of carriageway. Building it entailed wholesale destruction of the medieval core of Pest – the Old Town Hall was demolished and the Inner City Parish Church only escaped because of vociferous popular protest. *Buses 5, 7, 7A, 8, 8A.*

MARGIT HÍD (Margaret Bridge)

A French engineer, Ernest Gouin, designed the second bridge to be built (1876) after the Chain Bridge (see pages 82–3). To keep its two sections vertical to the current (divided at this point by Margaret Island) there is a 30-degree angle at the apex. A supplementary ramp (1900) leads down to the island. *Trams 4, 6; buses 6, 26, 91, 191.*

SZABADSÁG HÍD (Freedom Bridge)

An all-Hungarian effort in design and construction, this iron console bridge was inaugurated by Emperor Franz Joseph in 1896. The silver spike he ceremonially struck into the Pest abutment was stolen during the 1956 revolution. The Hungarian coat of arms is displayed on the central arches, topped by the mythic turul bird, supposed begetter of the Árpád dynasty. *Trams 1, 47, 49.*

Budavári Palota

(Royal Palace)

*F*ollowing the devastating Tartar invasions of 1240–1, King Béla IV decided to fortify the southern part of the Buda plateau, since the 11th century a defenceless agrarian settlement and part of 'Minor Pesth' (Lesser Pest).

The castle remained modest until Louis the Great of Anjou moved his court here from Visegrád, probably in 1347. His successor, Sigismund of Luxembourg (1387–1437), built a new L-shaped palace known as the 'Friss Palota' (New Palace). An indefatigable traveller, Sigismund scoured the courts of Europe for first-rate craftsmen whom he could lure to Buda. As the son of Charles IV of Bohemia, he must have employed artisans of the Parler workshop, responsible for the great cathedral of St Vitus in Prague. It was under Sigismund that various engineering projects were undertaken, including the building of a horse-driven pump to supply the palace with Danube water and the placing of a vast chain across the river to enforce the city's staple rights.

The Golden Age

The golden age of the court at Buda was that of King Matthias Corvinus (1458–90): his chapel was equipped with a water organ and his marvellous Bibliotheca Corviniana had 2,000 illuminated codices fastened to lecterns with golden chains. An army of craftsmen made beautiful ceramic stoves for the winter quarters, carved marble fireplaces and doorways, and gilded the coffered ceilings of sleeping chambers. Foreigners were duly impressed. An Italian wrote: 'In all Europe the three most beautiful cities are Venice on the sea, Buda on the hill and Florence on the plain.' Matthias's chief architect (resident in Buda between 1479 and 1491) was in fact a Florentine, Chimenti Camicia; another great contemporary architect, Giovanni Dalmata (a Dalmatian of Italian stock and builder of the magnificent cathedral of Sibenik) also worked for Europe's most glittering and ambitious monarch.

Decay and revival

During the 145-year-long Turkish occupation (1541–1686) the palace fell into decay. In 1678 lightning struck the gunpowder store, causing an explosion that destroyed most of Sigismund's palace. After the reconquest of Hungary by the Habsburgs and their allies, Charles VI's and Maria Theresa's

The Matthias Fountain on Castle Hill

architects razed much of the Gothic and Renaissance remnants and built a small baroque palace. No longer used as a royal residence – at different times it housed a convent and a university – it was eventually turned over to the Austrian Palatine (Viceroy) in 1790.

After being damaged in the 1848 War of Independence, the palace enjoyed its last flowering after the Compromise with Austria of 1867. Miklós Ybl, then Alajos Hauszmann, altered and considerably enlarged the baroque structure between 1869 and 1905. During the interwar period, the so-called Regent of Hungary, Admiral Horthy, installed himself here. In the closing days of World War II the whole place was reduced to rubble by the Russian bombardment. It has since been rebuilt incorporating some relics of the earlier palaces, but lacks the grace and splendour of its illustrious predecessors.

PALACE APPROACH

The Royal Palace can be approached from Szarvas tér in the south, reached by buses 86 (Buda side) and 78 (from Pest). Leaving the Southern Rondella on your right, you pass through the Ferdinand Gate, close to the menacing 'Mace Tower'. Access to the entrance to the Budapest History Museum is via walled gardens. From the north the palace may be reached using the *sikló* (funicular) from Clark Ádám tér, by bus 16 from Pest (Erzsébet tér) or by taking the *várbusz* (minibus) from Moszkva tér to Szent György tér.

The Lion Gate and rear courtyard of the Royal Palace complex, rebuilt after total devastation in World War II

One of the fine Gothic statues discovered in the Royal Palace foundations in 1974

BUDAPESTI TÖRTÉNETI MÚZEUM (Historical Museum of the City of Budapest)

Remnants of the Old Palace

Descend the stairway from the ticket office for a tour through the layers of the Renaissance and Gothic castle. At the entrance are the coats of arms of the Árpáds, the Anjous, Matthias Corvinus and the Jagiellon dynasties. Highlights of the tour include the Renaissance Hall, with a fragment of coffered ceiling in red marble by Giovanni Dalmata, an imposing marble fireplace and elegant reliefs of King Matthias and Queen Beatrice. You will also pass an ice-pit connected to the hanging garden above by a chute, and an area where the cistern was located. Further on are the former Queen's Quarters and the Royal Chapel of 1380 (the chapel's lower part was rededicated on 18 August 1990 as St Stephen's Chapel). There follows a spacious, partly Renaissance, hall where concerts are sometimes held.

Gothic statues from the Royal Palace

Along the corridor from the ticket counter a special display has been created for the beautiful Gothic statues unearthed during excavations in 1974. They were made during the reign of Sigismund of Luxembourg and appear to have been thrown into a builder's trench for use as rubble. Exactly why this happened is still a puzzle – perhaps the plans for the palace changed before they could be installed; or perhaps Sigismund's notoriously spendthrift ways finally caught up with him and unpaid workers indulged in a little iconoclasm.

The statues are dated to the third decade of the 15th century and fall into two categories, profane and sacred. Of the profane, some have lean elegant features, and could be members of the Anjou dynasty with their ladies and

MUSEUMS IN THE ROYAL PALACE COMPLEX

WING A: LUDWIG COLLECTION.
Open: Tuesday to Sunday
10am–6pm (sometimes to 4pm, may
be closed in winter).

WINGS B, C, D: MAGYAR NEMZETI
GALÉRIA (Hungarian National
Gallery)
Open: April to September, Tuesday to
Sunday 10am–6pm; October to
March to 4pm. Admission charge.
Free on Saturday. For an English-
speaking guide, ring the above
number and ask for extension 616.

WING E: BUDAPESTI TÖRTÉNETI
MÚZEUM (Historical Museum of the
City of Budapest)
Open: Wednesday to Monday 10am–
6pm (to 4pm between November and
March). Admission charge.
For the topographical and 19th
century part of the Budapest History
Museum, see Kiscelli Múzeum (pages
61 and 111).

WING F: ORSZÁGOS SZÉCHENYI
KÖNYVTÁR (Széchenyi National
Library)
Reading room open: Monday 1–9pm,
Tuesday to Saturday 9am–9pm.
Reader's ticket required. Occasional
exhibitions with differing opening
times. For a tour with an English-
speaking guide, ring the above
number and ask for extension 384.

Szent György tér 2. Tel: 175–7533.

contemporary knights and bishops.
Others in this category are fore-
shortened, suggesting that they were
placed high up; they have rounder, more
typically Magyar features. Figures in the
sacred series have been identified as
apostles or prophets.

The striking quality of these works is
eloquent testimony to the wealth of Buda
in the late Middle Ages, which could
afford to employ the best European
masters (probably Flemish and German,
but working in the French style).

History of Budapest
The rest of the museum is a rather old-
fashioned and less than inspiring
exhibition concerning the history and
development of Buda and Pest from the
Neanderthal period to the Romans
(second floor) and from the Romans to
the Magyar conquest (first floor). For the
subsequent history of Budapest, you
should visit the excellent Kiscelli
Museum in Óbuda (see page 61).

'Butter Churning' by Mihaly Munkascy

The former Legújabbkori Történeti Múzeum (Museum of Contemporary History) – now closed – documented the history of the working class movement in Hungary and was highly ideological. Its valuable photographic archives now belong to the National Gallery.

LUDWIG MÚZEUM (Ludwig Collection)

The building which housed the Museum of Contemporary History still contains a collection of modern art originally loaned, now donated, by the German industrialist Peter Ludwig. There are about 200 exhibits divided into two permanent displays: 'Art from the 1950s to the Present' and 'Hungarian Art from the 1960s to the Present'.

MAGYAR NEMZETI GALÉRIA (Hungarian National Gallery)

The 70,000 items of the National Gallery were moved to the reconstructed Royal Palace in 1975. Only Hungarian works (or those executed in Hungary) are displayed here (European masters and other antiquities may be found in the Museum of Fine Arts – see page 65).

Permanent displays

1 Medieval and Renaissance sculpture, including relics of the old Buda and Visegrád palaces – ground floor.
2 Gothic wooden sculpture and panel painting from the 14th to the 15th century, mostly from Upper Hungary (now Slovakia) – ground floor.
3 Late Gothic triptychs, including a celebrated *Annunciation* (1506) by Master MS – first floor.
4 Baroque art, dominated by Austrian artists who gained commissions in Hungary in the wake of the Counter-Reformation, but also containing interesting Hungarian portraits – first floor.
5 Hungarian painting and sculpture in the 19th century. Look out for the charming Biedermeier genre and landscape paintings by Miklós Barabás and the scenes from Hungarian history (eg works by Gyula Benczúr and Viktor Madarász) – first floor.

In another wing (first floor) are Hungarian Post-Impressionists and rooms devoted to the most successful Magyar painter ever, Mihály Munkácsy. His wide range includes the evocative *Dusty Road*, the melodramatic *Condemned Cell* and the amusing *Yawning Apprentice*.
6 Hungarian painting and sculpture of the 20th century. The highlights here are the dream-like work of Tivadar Csontváry Kosztka, the pointillism of József Rippl-Rónai, and, especially, the output of the *plein air* artists' colony at

Modern art show in the National Gallery

Nagybánya. Károly Ferenczy's *October* is perhaps the loveliest picture in the gallery – second floor.

The Palatine's Crypt
Every hour (usually) you can join a guided tour to see the marble-clad vaulted crypt and sarcophagus of the popular Palatine, Archduke Joseph of Habsburg.

MONUMENTS AROUND THE ROYAL PALACE

In front of the palace's main entrance is József Róna's 1900 equestrian statue of Prince Eugene of Savoy, the hero of the Turkish wars. Emperor Franz Joseph paid for its erection after the town that had commissioned it (Zenta) ran out of money.

To the north is Gyula Donáth's *Turul Bird* (1903), the mythical begetter of the Árpád line of kings. In the western courtyard is Alajos Stróbl's *Matthias Fountain*, a sculptural representation of a ballad by Mihály Vörösmarty, which tells the story of 'beautiful Ilonka', who met and fell in love with King Matthias when he was out hunting incognito. She pined away and died when she realised that her love was impossible.

Next to the fountain is György Vastagh's lively sculpture showing a *puszta* cowboy breaking in a horse.

ORSZÁGOS SZÉCHENYI KÖNYVTÁR (Széchenyi National Library)

The library was founded in 1802 by Count Ferenc Széchenyi, father of the great reform politician, István Széchenyi. By law it receives a copy of every Hungarian book or journal and also collects all scholarly works relating to Hungary.

Statue of Prince Eugene of Savoy, the Hammer of the Turks (above) and (below) the Turul Bird, mythical begetter of the Hungarian royal line

Churches

BELVÁROSI PLÉBÁNIA-TEMPLOM (Inner City Parish Church)

The history of Pest is reflected in the many-layered architecture of the Plébániatemplom. Succeeding a church built on the ruins of Roman *Contra-Aquincum*, a burial chapel for St Gellért was erected here in 1046. Parts of a subsequent 12th-century basilica survived Gothic reconstruction in the 15th century. The Turks turned the choir into a mosque, as a *mihrab* (prayer niche) in the south wall testifies. Baroque conversion under György Paur was begun in 1725 and two further alterations took place in the 19th century. Twentieth-century restorers have laid bare medieval details such as the sedilia in the sanctuary and the Italian-looking 15th-century fresco of the crucifixion.

The modern panels of the altar depicting the life of the Virgin Mary are the work of Pál C Molnár. At the end of the side aisle are two beautiful Renaissance tabernacles in red marble, probably made by craftsmen at the court of Matthias Corvinus. The statue of St Florian recalls fires that badly damaged Pest several times in the early 18th century (see also pages 114–15).
Március 15 tér 2. Tel: 318–3108. Metro to Ferenciek tere.

EGYETEMI TEMPLOM (University Church)

It is thought that the Dominicans had a church on this site in the Middle Ages, later turned into a mosque by the Turks. The Hungarian order of Paulites acquired it in the 1720s. Their church was not completed until 1742 (the towers 1770), and was probably designed by the Salzburg architect, Andreas Mayerhoffer.

The rococo ceiling frescos of the *Adoration of the Virgin* (1776) are by the Bohemian Johann Bergl, while the beautifully carved pews are the work of Paulite monks. The adjacent theological library also contains finely carved shelves and galleries, but may be difficult of access (see also page 113).
Egyetem tér 5–7/Papnövelde u. 7. Tel: 318–0555. Metro to Kálvin tér.

EVANGÉLIKUS TEMPLOM (Lutheran Church)

Emperor Joseph II's Tolerance Patent (1781) allowed the building of Protestant churches (but without towers) in areas where a minimum of 100 Protestant families existed to form a parish. The Lutheran Church of Pest, designed by Mihály Pollack, was completed by 1809 and József Hild added the neo-classical portico in 1856. The adjacent

The Inner City Parish Church

Evangélikus Országos Múzeum (Lutheran Museum) is also worth a visit: its most treasured possession is Martin Luther's will, acquired in 1804. Around four per cent of Hungarians are Lutherans.
Deák Ferenc tér 4. Tel: 117–4173. Museum open: Tuesday to Sunday 10am–6pm in summer, to 4pm in winter. Metro to Deák Ferenc tér.

FERENCIEK TEMPLOMA
(Franciscan Church)
The Italianate baroque church of the Franciscans in Pest was finished in 1758, but its Romantic tower was added in 1858. The 19th-century frescos of the interior are by Károly Lotz. A marked pew shows where the composer Franz Liszt used to sit.
Ferenciek tere 9. Tel: 317–3322. Metro to Ferenciek tere.

Ornamentation in the Inner City Parish Church (above) and the Óbuda Parish Church (left)

ÓBUDAI PLÉBÁNIA-TEMPLOM
(Óbuda Parish Church)
Károly Bebó is responsible for much of the notable interior of the charming baroque church of St Peter and St Paul in Óbuda. The carved pulpit is especially fine rococo work, with depictions of the Good Shepherd, Mary Magdalene and allegories of Faith, Hope and Charity.
Lajos utca 168. Tel: 368–6424. HÉV to Árpád híd.

The historic Matthias Church is dealt with in the section on Castle Hill (see pages 92–3). Some of the churches described below are also featured in the Walks (pages 102-23); these are cross-referenced.

REFORMÁTUS TEMPLOM
(Calvinist Church)

József Hofrichter's rigid neo-classical, somewhat provincial church of 1830 is not much enhanced by the portico added in 1838. The inside is more pleasing, with long galleries by József Hild and stained glass by Miksa Róth, the latter showing Protestant Hungarian heroes and Calvin himself. The treasury contains goldsmiths' work of the 17th to 19th centuries. (See pages 112–13.)
Kálvin tér 7. Tel: 217–6769. Metro to Kálvin tér.

SZENT ANNA-TEMPLOM
(St Anne's Church)

The original architect of the city's best loved baroque church (1761) is unknown, but the design is clearly Italianate. Above the doorway are sculptures representing Faith, Hope and Charity; further up are St Anne with Mary, the Buda coat of arms and a golden eye of God with angels. Inside, note the neo-baroque ceiling frescos by Pál C Molnár (1938) and the graceful pulpit by Károly Bebó.
Batthyány tér 7. Tel: 201–3404. Metro to Batthyány tér.

SZENT ISTVÁN-BAZILIKA
(St Stephen's Basilica)

Budapest debtors say 'I'll settle up when the Basilica is finished', an allusion to the 54 years (1851–1905) it took to build the church. After the dome of the neo-classical original collapsed (January 1868), Miklós Ybl rebuilt the church to a neo-Renaissance plan. Franz Joseph, attending the consecration, is said to have cast anxious eyes at the dome, whose previous fall, according to an eye-witness, made a 'horrible roar' and broke 300 windows in the neighbourhood. After Ybl's death József Kauser completed the work. St Stephen's is not basilical in form, but was granted basilical status by Pope Pius XI on the occasion of the Eucharistic Congress held in Budapest in 1938.

Ybl's replacement dome is one of the most striking features of the interior, 22m in diameter and 96m high. Leading academic artists of the day contributed to the church's decoration. Károly Lotz designed the dome mosaics, while Gyula Benczúr painted the popular *St Stephen Dedicating his Country to the Virgin Mary* (south transept). The marble statue of St Stephen on the high altar is by Alajos Stróbl.

The star attraction is the 'Szent Jobb',

St Anne's, one of the loveliest baroque churches in the city

claimed to be the mummified right hand of St Stephen (at the end of the passage to the left of the altar). In 1938 it was paraded round Hungary in a gold-painted train, but nowadays its excursions are limited to a circuit of the church on St Stephen's Day (20 August). See walk on pages 120–21.

Szent István tér 1. Tel: 317–2859. Metro to Deák Ferenc tér.

SZERB TEMPLOM
(Serbian Church)

The Serbian merchants and craftsmen of Pest had their own printing house and other institutions, including this attractive baroque church (1698). The architect is thought to have been Andreas Mayerhoffer. The iconostasis dates from 1850. Paintings of scenes from the life of Jesus, the saints and the apostles are by Károly Sterio (see page 113).

Szerb utca 2–4. Tel: 137–4230. Metro to Kálvin tér.

SZERVITAK TEMPLOMA
(Servite Church)

The Servites, one of the religious orders invited to Hungary during the Counter-Reformation, hung on in Pest, although the City Council once forced them to move, and on another occasion compelled them to rebuild on their own plot in a manner the Council thought fitting to the metropolis. Their church is in a pleasantly harmonious baroque style and contains some fine sculpture, notably János Thenny's statues of St Stephen, St Joachim, St Anne and St Ladislas (see also page 115).

Szervita tér 6. Tel: 318–5536. Metro to Deák Ferenc tér.

The façade of St Stephen's (above) and the magnificent dome

Gardens and Parks

EURÓPAPARK

This pleasant grove lies close to Ostrom utca below Bécsi kapu (Vienna Gate) on Castle Hill. In 1972, 100 years after the unification of Buda, Óbuda and Pest, the mayors from various cities round the world planted trees here, each of them a local symbol of growth and prosperity. There are 16 different species, among them Turkish hazel and Japanese cherry.
Várbusz from Moszkva tér to Bécsi kapu tér.

JUBILEUMI PARK, GELLÉRT-HEGY (Jubilee Park on Gellért Hill)

The Gellért Hill is criss-crossed with paths (see pages 106–7) that afford fine views of Pest. On the southwestern side of the hill, below the Citadella and the

Freedom Monument, the Jubilee Park was laid out in 1967 to mark the passage of 50 years since the Russian Revolution. The park is a delightful place for walking, with paths climbing from terrace to tree-lined terrace, green lawns, flower beds and children's play areas.
Gellért-hegy is reached by trams 47, 49.
Bus 86 to Szent Gellért tér.

MARGIT-SZIGET (Margaret Island)

Margit-sziget is named after Béla IV's daughter, who retired to a convent here and lived (according to her biographer) a life of exemplary piety. The Turks went to the other extreme, finding the sanctuary a conveniently secure place to keep the Pasha's harem. Palatine Joseph acquired possession in 1796, built a villa here and laid out a fine park with a rose garden. In 1869 it was opened to the public and became a favourite excursion area for Budapestians. The Habsburg governors sold it to the city in 1908. (See pages 108–9.)
Bus 26 from Nyugati pályaudvar.

NÉPLIGET (People's Park)

This now somewhat decayed park, the biggest in the capital, was laid out in the 1860s and much embellished with monuments, fountains and flower-beds at the time of the union of Buda and Pest. It includes the Budapest Planetarium and a laser theatre.
Metro to Népliget.

VÁROSLIGET (City Woodland Park)

See pages 96–7.

Budapest's parks are full of colour

BUDA

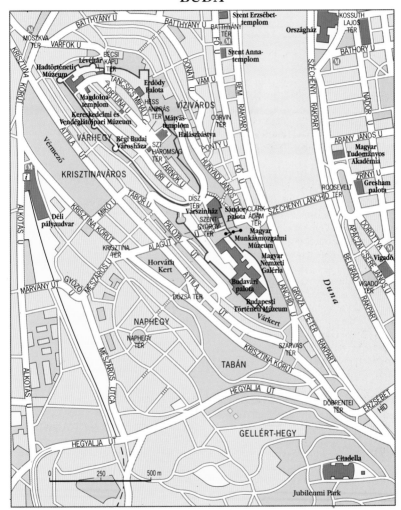

VÉRMEZŐ (Field of Blood)

The name of this grassy area west of Castle Hill recalls the fact that the leader of the Jacobin conspiracy of 1795, Ignác Martinovics, was executed here. The meadow covers the site of a medieval village.

Bus 5 from Március 15 tér.

The sepulchral chapel of Gül Baba

GÜL BABA TÜRBÉJE (Tomb of Gül Baba)

The only significant Turkish monument to survive in Budapest, other than baths, is the tomb of Gül Baba, situated in a sunken rose garden at the top of the cobbled Gül Baba utca on Rózsadomb.

Gül Baba was a dervish, a luminary of the Bektashi mendicant order whose members cultivated the arts and engaged in agriculture in time of peace, but were ready to die as martyrs (*ghazi*) in time of war. He died during a thanksgiving service for the conquest of Buda held in the Matthias Church (hastily trans-formed into a mosque) on Friday 2 September 1541. The Sultan himself is said to have been among the pallbearers as this distinguished Islamic scholar was

laid to rest. Hungarians later credited him with the introduction of rose cultivation in Hungary. Later still he entered popular mythology as a harmless figure of fun (he crops up in this role in an operetta by Jenő Huszka based on a story by Mór Jókai). The tomb was built on the orders of the Pasha between 1543 and 1548. It is a modest octagonal building with a hemispherical copper dome topped by a crescent moon. Originally this was a place of pilgrimage for pious Muslims and there was also a *tekke* (monastery) next to it. The Jesuits turned it into a chapel in 1689 and kept it until their dissolution in 1773. The Turkish government acquired the shrine in 1885 and donated some of the furniture – the rest has been given by Hungarian Muslims.

Mecset utca 14. Tel: 155–8849. Open: April to October, Tuesday to Sunday 10am–6pm, November to March 10am–4pm. Admission charge. Trams 4, 6 to Márgit hid, then a short walk.

KEREPESI TEMETŐ
(Kerepesi Cemetery)

Beyond the Eastern Railway Station (Keleti pályaudvar) Pest begins to spread itself with sports stadia, race tracks and the huge (90,000sq m) Kerepesi Cemetery. The cemetery, Hungary's national pantheon, is no longer in use. Its status as a patriotic shrine was scarcely enhanced by the inclusion of Communist worthies, buried with full honours traditionally supplied by the unsavoury 'Workers' Militia'. The last to be entombed in the 'Pantheon of the Working Class Movement' was János Kádár in 1989.

The simple tomb of the Dervish, Gül Baba

Kerepesi cemetery, last resting place of Hungarian heroes and villains

Perhaps it was the disagreeable company that prompted the son of László Rajk to have his father's remains removed from the area: Rajk Senior (who was just as unscrupulous as his tormentors, but spoke well) was executed after a show trial in 1949, Kádár himself having successfully obtained his 'confession' in prison. His rehabilitation and reburial in 1956 was attended by 250,000 and lit the fuse for the revolution of that year. Another notable absentee from Kerepesi is Imre Nagy, the ill-fated prime minister of 1956, who was reburied in the Pest Municipal Cemetery in 1989 after a ceremony in his honour on Heroes' Square. Previously he had lain in an unmarked grave.

Some distance from the burial place of those who enslaved their fellow-countrymen is that of Lajos Kossuth, who led them temporarily to freedom in 1848. The tomb is a rhetorical monument crowned by a figure holding aloft the torch of Liberty. Other major public figures who have graves of honour here include Lajos Batthyány (prime minister of the independent government of 1848), and Ferenc Deák (architect of the Compromise with Austria, 1867). József Antall, the first post-Communist prime minister, was buried here, next to Kossuth, on 18 December 1993. The world of the arts is represented by Ferenc Erkel, the actress Lujza Blaha, and Zsigmond Móricz (a turn-of-the-century writer in the Zola mould).

Main entrance in Fiumei út. Trams 23, 24, 36 from Keleti pályaudvar.

Hősök tere

(Heroes' Square)

*T*he 2.6km-long boulevard of Andrássy út ends in the east at Heroes' Square, the site chosen at the end of the last century for the millennial memorial.

Every monument on the square relates to the theme of national identity along with the triumphs and catastrophes of Magyar history.

MILLENNIUMI EMLÉKMŰ

In the vast square that confronts you as you enter from the west, the dominant object is György Zala's 36m-high Millennium Monument. At the top of an elegant Corinthian column is a representation of the Archangel Gabriel, holding the Crown of St Stephen in one hand and the Apostolic Cross in the other. According to legend, the Archangel appeared to King Stephen in a dream and told him to convert the Hungarians to Christianity. The Apostolic or Patriarchal Cross (with two horizontal bars) signifies King Stephen's role as converter of the nation.

At the base of the column are Zala's romantic representations of the leaders of the seven Magyar tribes who entered the Carpathian Basin in AD896. The depiction of these fearsome-looking chieftains astride their horses represents the apotheosis of romantic historicism

Statue of István Bocskai, the pantheon on Heroes' Square

at the turn of the century. In front of the column and the seven chieftains is a simple memorial to the Hungarian soldiers who fell in two world wars, with a guard of honour on political anniverseries.

THE COLONNADE

Behind the Archangel Gabriel column is a crescent-shaped colonnade with statues of significant figures in Hungarian history placed above friezes showing crucial historical events. From left to right the statues represent: St Stephen, St Ladislas, Kálmán Könyves (Beauclerc), Andrew II and Béla IV (all of the Árpád dynasty); the Angevin rulers Charles Robert and Louis the Great; János Hunyadi (Regent 1445–52) and Matthias Corvinus; then four Transylvanian princes (replacing Habsburgs – see page 54); and finally the 19th-century revolutionary leader Lajos Kossuth (see page 73). Above are allegorical sculptures of War and Peace, Work and Wealth, Knowledge and Glory.

PEST

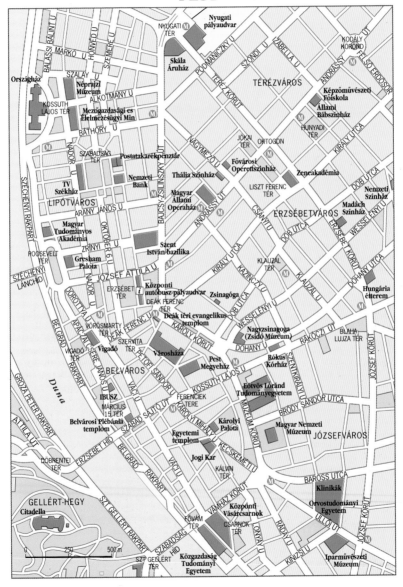

THE MILLENNIAL CELEBRATIONS

In 1881 the Budapest Council submitted a proposal to the National Assembly for a monument to mark the arrival of the Hungarians in the Carpathian Basin some 1,000 years earlier. Scholars were unable to agree on the exact date of this event, unhelpfully reporting back that it was not before 888 and not after 900. In the end a millennium of 1896 was chosen. György Zala and Albert Schickedanz were entrusted with preparing a monumental scheme that should, in the words of historian András Gerő, help to 'construct an integrated national and historical ideology' and 'inspire a sense of continuity and permanence'.

The statues and monuments were actually erected after the Millennial Celebrations (for which the first stretch of underground railway was also built). The 1896 exhibition celebrating Magyar achievements took up the whole area of the Városliget (see pages 96–7) and was approached by a triumphal arch on Heroes' Square. It attracted over six million visitors.

Symbolism and Politics on Heroes' Square

After the Ausgleich (Compromise) with Austria in 1867, a degree of sovereignty was at last restored to Hungary after centuries of absolute rule from Vienna. But the fact that the King-Emperor (Franz Joseph) was still a Habsburg posed delicate problems for those constructing a monument to national achievement which, on the one hand, had to make concessions to Magyar pride, and on the other had to avoid any offence to the ruling house.

Habsburg rule effectively began in 1526 following defeat by the Turks at the Battle of Mohács. In dealing with the period before this, national glory under native and foreign dynasties could be confidently asserted – sometimes providing a salutary historical reminder for the Habsburgs at the same time. An example is the frieze under the colonnade statue of Charles Robert of Anjou which depicts the battle of the Marchfeld (1278); it was here that Rudolf of Habsburg's victory over Ottakar of Bohemia was secured by the Hungarian king, Ladislas IV, and his Cumanian cavalry.

Originally the colonnade contained the statues of five Habsburgs: Ferdinand I, Charles VI, Maria Theresa, Leopold II and Franz Joseph himself. These were generally the ones least offensive to Hungarian sensitivities, or even, like Maria Theresa, held in some affection.

Relief of battling Hungarians on Heroes' Square

Under the Communist Republic of Councils (1919) the Habsburg statues were removed and the Millennium Monument turned into a giant obelisk, the front of which featured Karl Marx being fawned upon by grateful workers. Under the Regent, Miklós Horthy, the Habsburgs were returned to their niches, but were once again removed by the Communists after World War II, to be replaced by the independent Transylvanian princes of the 17th and 18th centuries, István Bocskai, Gábor Bethlen, Imre Thököly and Ferenc Rákóczi.

The Rákosi regime would have liked to sweep away the whole monument, since its symbolism was not appropriate to their historical script.

The pantheon of great Hungarians (above) and the façade of the Museum of Fine Arts (below)

MŰCSARNOK (Hall of Art)

Schickedanz and Herzog were the architects for the building on the south side of Heroes' Square, the Hellenistic Műcsarnok (1895). It proved useful during World War I, when it was requisitioned as a military hospital. The mosaic on the pediment, *St Stephen as Patron of the Arts*, was a later addition. The gallery mostly shows work by modern Hungarian artists.

SZÉPMŰVÉSZETI MÚZEUM (Museum of Fine Arts)

On the north side of Heroes' Square is the gallery devoted to non-Hungarian art (see page 65). This imposing piece of Hellenistic historicism (1906) was also designed by Zala's co-worker on the Millennium project, Albert Schickedanz, with Fülöp Herzog.
Dózsa György üt 37.

Hősök tere is reached from Vörösmarty tér with the metro (földalatti – yellow line).

Jugendstil Architecture

*I*n Central Europe the German term 'Jugendstil' is applied to the art nouveau architecture that had its roots in the Paris of the 1890s. In Budapest the word *szecesszió* – 'Secession style' – is also used, reflecting the influence of the famous Vienna Secession movement, established in 1897 in opposition to the conservative and academic elements that prevailed in the arts.

Jugendstil/art nouveau was a liberating force, sensual, richly ornamental and prepared to draw eclectically on the world of nature and folklore for its motifs. Coming, as it did, with the upsurge of national consciousness in the

The gable mosaic of the former Turkish Bank

countries of the Austro-Hungarian Empire, it is not surprising that idiosyncratic versions arose at local level.

Hungarian Jugendstil drew on current ideas about ethnic roots; in the works of Ödön Lechner this was carried further and developed into a so-called 'national style' (see pages 58–9). However, all Jugendstil architects, whether leaning towards the approach of Lechner, or that

of the Viennese Secession, or even that of the English Arts and Crafts movement, shared a common enthusiasm for exploiting materials such as ceramics, glass and wrought iron; a determination to avoid pattern-book repetition of forms was another characteristic principle. Though in public buildings individuality sometimes had to give way to official or commercial considerations, private villas for the wealthy (of which the vast majority were built at the turn of the century) provided an opportunity for architects to give free rein to their imagination and ingenuity.

Anyone interested in seeing some of these private houses should wander around either side of the outer reaches of Andrássy út. Examples of fine Jugendstil villas can be seen at Városligeti fasor 24 and 33, both designed by Emil Vidor; further out, at Ajtósi Dürer sor 25, is the villa built for the sculptor György Zala (co-organiser of the Millennium memorial project), to a modified Lechner design.

JUGENDSTIL BUILDINGS

Although Ödön Lechner and his partner, Gyula Pártos (see pages 58–9) over-shadow the rest, there were many interesting architects in turn-of-the-century Budapest who built their own more or less idiosyncratic versions of Jugendstil. Their public and commercial buildings are all near the centre of Pest.

GRESHAM PALOTA (Gresham Palace)

This richly ornamented but crumbling block was built for the English insurance company of the same name by Zsigmond Quittner between 1905 and 1907. It has splendid stairways, stained glass by the Gödöllő artist, Miksa Róth, and a marvellous wrought-iron gate with peacock motifs.
Roosevelt tér 5. Buses 4, 16.

PÁRIZSI UDVAR (Paris Arcade)

Henrik Schmahl's 1911 arcade has elaborate ornamentation on the façade as well as inside, where the coloured glass lights in the roof create an atmosphere of Alhambra-like mystery.
Ferenciek tere 5. Blue metro to Ferenciek tere.

TÖRÖK BANKHÁZ (former Turkish Bank)

The glassed façade of the house (Henrik Böhm, Ármin Hegedüs, 1906) recalls French art nouveau. Miksa Róth made the striking mosaic in the gable, showing the Magyars offering allegiance to the Virgin Mary in her capacity as *Patrona Hungariae.*
Szervita tér 3. Metro to Deák Ferenc tér.

On the same square Béla Lajta's **Rózavölgyi Ház** (no 5) betrays the influence of the controversial Viennese architect, Adolf Loos. There is another Jugendstil façade at no 2.

TOMB OF THE SCHMIDL FAMILY

It is worth the long trek to the Jewish Cemetery in Kőbánya to see the loveliest combined effort of Ödön Lechner and Béla Lajta, a gleaming gem of green and turquoise ceramic with gold edging, setting off delicate floral and star motifs. Inside is a stylised mosaic of the Tree of Life.
Izraelita temető, Kozma utca. Tram 37 (long journey) from Népszínház utca.

The Gresham Palace – in need of a face-lift, but a fine building

Hungarian National Style

'*H*ungarian form did not exist – but it will now!' With these auspicious words Ödön Lechner (1845–1914) began his idiosyncratic quest for a national style. His remark echoes and complements a similar declaration by Count István Széchenyi in 1830: 'Many people think "Hungary once was": I want to believe "she will be".'

Lechner spent some years abroad, and English and French influences are present in his early work. When Jugendstil/art nouveau arrived in Hungary, he embraced it enthusiastically. In a whimsical interpretation of ethnic roots he happily incorporated Indian, Persian and Moorish motifs, together with ornamentation derived from Hungarian folk art.

Magisterially indifferent to mere technical details of weight or stress, which he left to his long-suffering partners (notably Gyula Pártos), Lechner was equally cavalier about expense – or so his enemies in the city council claimed (in the end they managed to prevent him getting any more commissions). For his part Lechner pointed out that he used brick, which was cheaper than the stone used by his main rival, and majolica, which was easier to clean. When asked why he ornamented the backs of roofs, which could not be seen, he replied: 'Why shouldn't the birds have something to enjoy?'

LECHNER BUILDINGS

IPARMŰVÉSZETI MÚZEUM
(Museum of Applied Arts)

The restored Moorish-style stucco of the interior is supurb. The stairwell's tiers of undulating carved banisters are topped by an attractive stained-glass cupola.
Üllői út 33–37. Tel: 217–5222. Metro to Kálvin tér.

Detail from Ödön Lechner's fine Post Office Savings Bank

Major works by Lechner: the Museum of
Applied Art (above), the Post Office Savings
Bank (right) and the Geology Institute (below)

MAGYAR ÁLLAMI FÖLDTANI INTÉZET (Institute for Geology)

Pale yellow walls, strips of brown
brickwork and a light blue ceramic roof
topped by a huge globe make this one of
Lechner's most eye-catching buildings.
*Stefánia út 14. Tel: 251–0999. Metro to
Népstadion, then trolley-bus 75.*

POSTATAKARÉKPÉNZTÁR (Post Office Savings Bank)

The walls rise to crenellations of yellow
majolica; beyond these is a roof with
coloured hexagonal tiles, richly
ornamented with floral motifs, angel-
wings, dragons' tails and other exotica.
The recurrent representations of bee and
honeycomb (originally also reflected in
the fittings of the interior) symbolise the
bank's activity (see page 119).
Hold utca 4. Bus 15 to Szabadság tér.

Museums

Many of Budapest's more than 40 museums are in buildings of architectural interest (eg the Ethnographical Museum, see page 65). The most important are described here, while others are featured in the walks (see pages 102–23). Museums in the complex of the Budavári palota (Royal Castle) are dealt with on pages 38–43. Many museums have free admission one day in the week – the day varies, so telephone first if you want to take advantage of this.

HADTÖRTÉNETI MÚZEUM
(Museum of Military History)
Based in the former Palatine Barracks on Castle Hill, the display includes rooms devoted to the War of Independence (1848–9), World War I and the 1956 revolution.

Toth Árpád sétany 40. Tel: 356–9522. Open: Tuesday to Saturday 10am–5pm, Sunday 10am–6pm. Admission charge. Várbusz from Moszkva tér to Bécsi kapu tér.

IPARMŰVÉSZETI MÚZEUM
(Museum of Applied Arts)
The Jugendstil museum was built by Ödön Lechner with Gyula Pártos in

Earthenware vase (above) and figurine (below) in the Museum of Applied Arts

1896 (see page 58). The opening, attended by Franz Joseph himself, was part of the Millennial Celebration of that year (see page 54). Its oriental style of ornamentation reflected the architect's view that Magyars had originally come from the Far East.

A permanent exhibition showing stylistic development from the 12th century to the present opened in the mid-1990s and is gradually changed to present different aspects of the collection.

Üllői út 33–7. Tel: 217–5222. Open: Tuesday to Sunday 10am–6pm. Admission charge. Metro to Ferenc körút. Trams 4, 6 to Üllői út.

KISCELLI MÚZEUM
(Kiscell Museum)

The most enjoyable of Budapest's history museums chronicles the ages of the city in displays combining nostalgia with scholarship. A section on printing shows the machine that printed Sándor Petőfi's 'National Song', which roused the populace in the 1848 revolution. It is also worth lingering over the paintings, mostly by 19th- and turn-of-the-century Hungarian masters.

Kiscelli utca 108. Tel: 388–8560. Open: summer, Tuesday to Sunday 10am–6pm, (4pm in winter). Admission charge (Wednesdays free). Tram 17, buses 60, 165 to Kiscelli utca.

KÖZLEKEDÉSI MÚZEUM
(Museum of Transport)

Gerbeaud label in the Museum of Catering

The origin of the collection lies in the Millennial Exhibition of 1896 (see page 54). Features include the history of the Hungarian railway, historic vehicles and urban, water and road transportation. In the Petőfi Hall near by is a permanent display on the history of aviation. The museum has two outlying branches: the Kossuth Ship Museum (anchored next to the Chain Bridge on the Pest side) and the Földalatti Múzeum (Museum of the Underground Railway) in the Deák Ferenc tér metro station.

Városligeti körút 11. Tel: 343–0565. Open: Tuesday to Friday 10am–5pm, Saturday and Sunday 10am–6pm. Admission charge. Trolley buses 72, 74 to Hermina út.

MAGYAR KERESKEDELMI ÉS VENDÉGLÁTÓIPARI MÚZEUM
(Museum of Commerce and Catering)

The emphasis here is on everything to do with the catering and retail grocery trade. The re-created interiors of 19th-century food shops have great charm and attractive period posters are on sale.

Fortuna utca 4. Tel: 375–6249. Open: Tuesday to Sunday 10am–6pm. Admission charge. Várbusz from Moszkva tér to Szentháromság tér.

MAGYAR MEZŐGAZDASÁGI MÚZEUM (Agricultural Museum)

This educational museum is another legacy of the millennial show. Of the 18 permanent displays, those on wine production, animal husbandry and fishing are perhaps the most interesting. Horse breeding, also featured, is another field where Count István Széchenyi was active, importing English horses and methods to Hungarian studs and instituting the first horse races.

The museum is housed in the baroque part of the Vajdahunyad Castle on Széchenyi-sziget, Olof Palme sétany, Városliget. Tel: 343–3198. Open: Tuesday to Saturday 10am–4pm, Sunday 10am–5pm. Admission charge. Metro to Hősök tere.

Magyar Nemzeti Múzeum
(Hungarian National Museum)

COUNT FERENC SZÉCHENYI (1754–1820)

The story of the Hungarian National Museum begins with Ferenc Széchenyi, father of 'the greatest Hungarian', István Széchenyi, and like him a patriot and moderniser. Emperor Joseph II appointed him Viceroy of Croatia, but Széchenyi realised that Joseph's centralising and authoritarian approach left no room for national aspirations and resigned his post in 1786. He devoted himself to collecting artefacts and books with a view to donating them to the Hungarian nation; but even this gesture had to receive permission from Joseph's successor, Franz I, before it could be put into effect.

In his old age Széchenyi became fanatically conservative and seems to have suffered from religious melancholy, foreshadowing the mental instability that overtook his son in his final years.

Foundation of the National Museum

The Széchenyi collection consisted of 11,884 documents, 1,150 manuscripts, 142 volumes of maps and engravings and 2,675 coins. It was valued at the then enormous sum of 160,000 *forints* and constituted in 1802 the third most important national museum in Europe (after the Louvre and the British Museum). The museum enjoyed the support of the Palatine, Archduke Joseph, who became one of the trustees.

Expansion was at first hampered by application of an archaic law under which all objects discovered on Hungarian soil belonged to 'the state' and were transferred to Vienna. Then, in 1832, the great collection of the scholar Miklós Jankovich was acquired, marking the 'second founding' of the museum. At the same time the Palatine persuaded the Diet to allocate half a million *forints* (to come from the pockets of the nobility) for the construction of an edifice sufficiently splendid to be the repository of the nation's heritage.

Statue of the poet János Arany

The museum

The leading neo-classical architect of the day, Mihály Pollack, was chosen to design the building, which was completed in 1837. Its façade recalls the Erechtheion on the Athens Acropolis, while the interior stairway sweeps up to a domed area reminiscent of the Pantheon in Rome.

The collection is divided into sections covering archaeology, the history of the Hungarian people and the coronation insignia (crown, orb,

ST STEPHEN'S CROWN

A whole room is devoted to the royal insignia and the historic 'Holy Crown' (which actually post-dates the reign of St Stephen). It was returned to Hungary in 1978 from America, where it had been since the end of World War II. The crown is that of a Byzantine empress (*corona graeca*) to which an upper part (*corona latina*) was added, perhaps under Béla III (1172–96). The famous leaning cross on the top replaced an earlier one, a reliquary probably containing a fragment of the True Cross. The *corona graeca* features portraits of the Byzantine Emperor Michael Ducas, flanked by his son and the Hungarian King Géza I (1074–7). The precious stones symbolise the four elements – sapphire for air, almandine (a kind of garnet) for fire, green glass for earth and the rim of pearls for water.

chasuble, sceptre and sword – see above). Highlights include a room devoted to the 1848 revolution, the tent of a Turkish commander and Renaissance stalls with beautiful marquetry from the church at Nyírbátor (northeast Hungary). The panelled Széchenyi Memorial Room contains a portrait of the founder by the Viennese artist, Joseph Ender; round the top of the walls are the coats of arms of all the Hungarian counties.

The moth-eaten natural history collection on the top floor is in the process of being modernised.
Múzeum körút 14–16. Tel: 338–2122. Open: Tuesday to Sunday 10am–6pm. Admission charge. Metro to Kálvin tér.

The Royal insignia

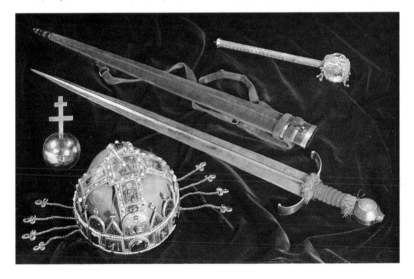

Museums

BARTÓK EMLÉKHÁZ
(Béla Bartók Memorial House)

The composer Béla Bartók (1881–1945) lived in this villa from 1932 until his escape from Hungary in 1940. In the garden is a life-size statue of him by Imre Varga. Bartók's furniture has been reinstated in the rooms, together with some of his collection of Hungarian ceramics and textiles. The former living room, with its painted wooden ceiling, is used for concerts.

Csalán út 29. Tel: 394–2100. Open: Tuesday to Sunday 10am–5pm. Admission charge. Bus 5 to Pasaréti tér, then 10 minutes' walk.

Anyone interested in Bartók's collaborator in the work of collecting Hungarian folk music can visit the Kodály Zoltán Emlékmúzeum (Zoltan Kodály Memorial Museum – address on page 122).

Interior of Béla Bartók's house

LISZT FERENC EMLÉKMÚZEUM
(Franz Liszt Memorial Museum)

The former apartment of Franz Liszt contains photographs and documents illustrating the composer's stormy life (1811–86). Liszt's books, musical scores and much of his furniture have been preserved and there is a bronze of the great man's right hand by Alajos Stróbl. *Vörösmarty utca 35. Tel: 322–9804. Open: Monday to Friday 10am–6pm, Saturday 9am–5pm. Admission charge. Metro to Vörösmarty utca.*

MTA ZENETÖRTÉNETI MÚZEUM
(Museum of the History of Music)

Housed in the baroque Erdődy Palace on Castle Hill, the collection has over 1,500 instruments, photographs and musical documents. On the ground floor the permanent display deals with the manufacture of musical instruments, 18th- and 19th-century musical life and Hungarian folk music. On the first floor is an archive of Bartók's manuscripts.

Táncsics Mihály utca 7. Tel: 375–9011.
Open: 15 March to 15 November, Monday
3–6pm, Wednesday to Sunday 10am–5pm.
Admission charge. Várbusz from Moszkva
tér to Bécsi kapu tér.

NÉPRAJZI MÚZEUM
(Ethnographical Museum)
This museum is worth visiting to view the
neo-Renaissance interior of Alajos
Hauszmann's building (1896). It began life
as Hungary's Supreme Court, hence
Károly Lotz's emblematic fresco on the
ceiling of Justitia enthroned among the
clouds, flanked by allegories of Justice,
Peace, Sin and Revenge.

The first floor is devoted to the
traditional culture of the peoples of
Hungary and was opened only in 1991. On
the second floor, with the help of material
from the museum's marvellous
photographic archive, primitive cultures are
documented, including that of the Ob-
Ugrian Hanti and Manszi tribes in the
Urals, ancestral relatives of the Hungarians.
Kossuth Lajos tér 12 Tel: 332–6340. Open:
Tuesday to Sunday 10am–6pm (4pm
December to Febraury). Admission charge.
Metro to Kossuth Lajos tér.

SEMMELWEIS ORVOSTÖRTÉNETI
MÚZEUM (Semmelweis Museum of
Medicine)
Named after Ignác Semmelweis
(1818–65), the 'Saviour of Mothers' (see
page 106), whose father had a grocery
shop here, the museum has a fascinating
display of medicine from its beginnings in
the ancient world to the present. There is
also a complete neo-classical pharmacy
designed by Mihály Pollack.
Apród utca 1/3. Tel: 375–3533. Open:
Tuesday to Sunday 10.30am–5.30pm.
Admission charge. Buses 86, 5, 78 to
Szarvas tér. Tram 19.

Window in the Ethnographical Museum

SZÉPMŰVÉSZETI MÚZEUM
(Museum of Fine Arts)
This is one of Europe's most substantial
art collections with 2,500 paintings on
display, many derived from the Esterházy
Collection purchased by the Hungarian
state in 1870. The Italian school is
particularly well represented and there
are no less than five striking El Grecos.
Dózsa György út 41. Tel: 343–9759.
Open: Tuesday to Sunday 10am–6pm
(4pm January to March). Admission
charge. Metro to Hősök tere.

The Museum of Fine Arts

Music Venues

ÚJ SZÍNHÁZ
(New Theatre – formally Parisiana)

This gem of theatre architecture was built as a cabaret by Béla Lajta in 1909. Alterations in the 1920s transformed Lajta's original Jugendstil into something closer to art deco. Its complete renovation won the 1998 Europe Nostra Prize and has resulted in a glittering array of gilding, glasswork and coloured marble. *Paulay Ede utca 35. Tel: 269–6021. Metro, yellow line (földallati) to Opera.*

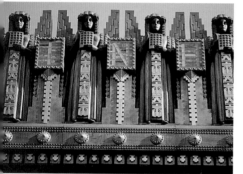

The New Theatre

ERKEL SZÍNHÁZ (Erkel Theatre)

Renovation has left little of the building's original Jugendstil ornamentation intact, but its modern styling is itself attractive. In particular, the first-floor buffet area boasts two spectacular wall paintings by the Hungarian painter, Aurél Bernáth. At one end is *A Midsummer Night's Dream* and at the other a representation of Imre Madách's Faustian drama *The Tragedy of Man* (1861). Bernáth worked on the paintings between 1972 and 1973. *Köztársaság tér 30. Tel: 333–0540. Metro (red line) to Blaha Lujza tér.*

FERENC ERKEL (1810–93)

First director of the National Theatre, Erkel composed the quintessential Hungarian opera *Bánk Bán* (1861), a musical setting of József Katona's patriotic play about a murder at the medieval Hungarian court. Erkel's music combined elements of the 18th-century *verbunkos* (played on recruiting drives), folk themes and pre-Verdian opera. He also wrote the remarkably moving Hungarian national anthem (1844).

MAGYAR ÁLLAMI OPERAHÁZ
(Hungarian State Opera)

In the 1870s it was decided to build an opera house in Pest of comparable grandeur to those in other European cities. Miklós Ybl won the commission and the opera house went up between 1875 and 1884. Built in a graceful neo-Renaissance style, the technically sophisticated building embodies national pride combined with allusions to musical history. In niches either side of the main entrance are statues of Hungary's two greatest 19th-century composers: Ferenc Erkel (left) and Ferenc (Franz) Liszt (right). Four Muses are represented at the corners of the first storey, while famous composers line the balustrade above. The interior was decorated by Bertalán Székely, Mór Than and Károly Lotz (note Lotz's cupola fresco of Apollo on Olympus). Technical innovations included new fire precautions, several European theatres having recently burned down with loss of life. It was also something of a feat to install the

The Operetta Theatre

auditorium's bronze chandelier weighing all of three tonnes. The cost ran to one million *forints*, most of it personally contributed by Emperor Franz Joseph.

Famous directors of the opera include Gustav Mahler (1888–91), Arthur Nikisch (1893–95) and Otto Klemperer (1947–50). In the 1930s (surprisingly, in view of the right-wing political climate) a number of modern operas were staged, including works by Stravinsky. The detailed history of the opera house is presented in a small display on the first floor (Székely room), accessible during the intervals.

Andrássy út 22. Tel: 331–2550. Metro, földallati (yellow line) to Opera.

The National Opera, one of the most graceful works of Miklós Ybl

MIKLÓS YBL (1814–91)

The opera is probably the finest work of this great Hungarian architect, one of the best practitioners of so-called historicism (architecture that draws inspiration from the styles of previous eras). He built many noble apartment blocks in Pest, constructed around an internal courtyard and offering spacious, high-ceilinged flats for the well-to-do. His public works reflect the grandeur and elegance of the Italian Renaissance. They include the second phase of St Stephen's Basilica and the huge Customs House (now the University of Economics). A statue of Ybl stands on the Danube bank below the castle, opposite his Várbazár complex (see page 106).

The Vigadó (Concert Hall)

PESTI VIGADÓ (The Pest Concert Hall)

Mihály Pollack's original 'redoute' (ball-room) on this site fell victim to Austrian cannon fire from the Buda Hill during the 1848–9 War of Independence. Between 1858 and 1865 Frigyes Feszl built a new concert hall in a romantic style that incorporates oriental elements, reflecting the Asiatic roots of the Magyars: one of the figures in the frieze along the top of the façade is Attila the Hun, though the descent of the Hungarians from the Huns is more than doubtful. Further emphasis is placed on Magyar identity by the interior frescoes, scenes from Hungarian folk tales painted by Károly Lotz and Mór Than. 'Vigadó' is coined from '*vigad*', to make merry – or have a ball – and the place has never lost its ballroom function (balls are still held here during Shrovetide Carnival). Károly Alexy's dancing figures on the façade are thus absolutely appropriate. *Vigadó tér 1–2. Tel: 318–9167. Tram 2 along the Pest embankment to Vigadó tér.*

ZENEAKADÉMIA (Music Academy)

The first music academy was founded in 1875 by Franz Liszt and occupied three rooms above his flat in Irányi utca (Pest); there were then 38 students of piano and composition. After four years, demand was such that expansion became necessary, and the academy moved to Andrássy út (then Sugár út), where it occupied several floors and had its first auditorium. At the turn of the century the city decided to buy land for a much bigger music conservatory, subsequently built between 1904 and 1907 to plans by Flóris Korb and Kálmán Giergl.

The Liszt Ferenc Zeneművészeti Főiskola (Franz Liszt High School for Music), to give it its official title, is a remarkable example of Korb and Giergl's idiosyncratic style, sometimes called 'Baroque Jugendstil'. Liszt is honoured with a huge statue (by Alajos Stróbl) over the main entrance and there are reliefs of two other founding professors, Ferenc Erkel and Róbert Volkmann. The building's exterior is pompous and heavy, but the interior is striking, particularly in the iridescent colours of the Zsolnay ceramic fittings. In the first floor lobby is Aladár Körösfői-Kriesch's weird fresco *The Fountain of Youth*, with the sententious inscription: 'Those who search for life make a pilgrimage to the well-spring of art'. Its painter was a member of the artists' colony based in the village of Gödöllő, north of Budapest, whose members drew inspiration from Hungarian folk motifs and the English Pre-Raphaelites. Above the entrances to the auditorium on the ground floor Körösfői-Kriesch has painted two further frescos representing sacred and profane music.

The large auditorium of the Music Academy seats 1,200 and is famous for its excellent acoustics. On the walls are images (painted by István Gróh and Ede Telcs) suggesting musical movements –

Allegro, Andante, Adagio and Scherzo. The smaller auditorium is used for chamber music and seats 400. The foyer has frescos by János Zichy illustrating Hungarian musical history.

The Academy has had a distinguished past: many world famous performers such as Antal Doráti, George Szell and Sir Georg Solti are numbered among its pupils. Its professors included all the great Hungarian composers: Ferenc Erkel, Béla Bartók, Zoltán Kodály, Leó Weiner and, of course, Liszt himself. The musical tradition here is unbroken, except for a bizarre interlude at the end of World War II when the building was used for the trial of Ferenc Szálasi, the Hungarian fascist leader and psychopath.
Liszt Ferenc tér 8. Tel: 341–4788. Trams 4 and 6 to Király utca.

Körösfői-Kriesch, fresco in the Music Academy

OPERETTA

Operetta was very popular during the period of the Austro-Hungarian Empire (1867–1918). Its origins were various: Austrian composers were inspired by the smash hits of Jacques Offenbach in Paris and by the tradition of the Wiener Volksstück (Viennese Popular Theatre). The Hungarian equivalent of the latter was the 'Népszínmű'. A musical rendering of Sándor Petőfi's poem about the life and love of a peasant boy from the Great Plain (*János Vitéz*) is a classic example of it. The characteristic figures represented in Hungarian 'Népszínmű' became the romantic clichés associated with a world that was already passing: the *csikós* (cowboy from the Great Plain), the *betyár* (a sort of Robin Hood), the *husar* (hussar), the *táblabíró* (provincial judges with feudal attitudes), together with a cast of peasants, 'heyducks' (personal gendarmerie of the magnates) and sentimentally portrayed gypsies.

The classic operetta is Johann Strauss's *Die Fledermaus* (1874), a witty and melodious satire on the decadent world of late 19th-century Vienna. The more strait-laced public in Budapest were initially slow to accept this, but then came the *Gypsy Baron* (1885), a work that symbolically united the two halves of the Empire.

Scenes from operetta

The libretto was based on a story by the greatest Hungarian novelist, Mór Jókai, and Johann Strauss wrote the music. It was an instant success.

The final period of operetta, which was increasingly a vehicle of escape from the realities of imperial decline and war, was dominated by Hungarian composers. Ferenc Lehár wrote two works that conquered the world (*The Merry Widow*, 1905 and *Land of Smiles*, 1929). The prolific Emmerich Kálmán had an enormous success with the *Csárdás Princess* (1915). The

frenetic energy and brittle glamour of its dance routines, set in the nightclub milieu, seem in retrospect to be the dance of death of the Empire itself:

'Every pulse is racing faster
While we dance and flirt and play:
The world outside is all disaster;
What care we till break of day...?'

See page 147 for details of operetta highlights played through the summer at the Pesti Vigadó.

Ország ház
(Parliament)

The Parliamentary tradition

Feudalism endured in Hungary right up to the 19th century, in some respects even into the 20th. The first glimmerings of modern parliamentarianism are contained in a memorandum submitted to the 1790–1 session of the Diet by a legal historian, József Hajnóczy. Leading politicians of the Reform Era (István Széchenyi, Ferenc Deák, József Eötvös) advocated a widening and loosening of

Interior of the Parliament

'If I were the ruler of Hungary, I would order all ships passing by on the Danube to stop for two minutes in front of the Houses of Parliament, so that travellers on board can admire, enjoy and learn from the beauty of the best Hungarian building.'
JOZSEF KESZLER, writing in *Magyar Nemzet* when the Parliament was completed in 1902.

noble privilege, and the revolutionary government of 1848 actually raised the proportion of the population enjoying political rights from 2.5 per cent to 8 per cent. The franchise was effectively narrowed again through tax qualifications in the 1870s and it was not until 1918 that universal suffrage briefly arrived. The Horthy period (partially) and Communism (totally) eclipsed democracy although in between free elections were held in 1947. The present government is the second to be democratically elected after the 43 years of totalitarianism and the fourth in Hungary's history.

The building of the Parliament

A competition to design the proposed Parliament building was held in 1883. Only 19 plans were submitted (in contrast to the Berlin Reichstag, which attracted 180 entries); the small number may have been due to the specifications. Imre Steindl (1839–1902) won with a neo-Gothic design, attacked by some as a 'German style', alien to the Hungarians; its supporters pointed out that Magyar and German culture had interacted fruitfully for centuries. In its style, river position and cruciform layout the building showed the influence of Barry and Pugin's new Palace of Westminster on the Thames in London. The exterior presents a dazzling array of finials, buttresses, towers and a mighty dome. The gilded, marble-clad interior lives up to its role as a national shrine. In the Speaker's Hall is Mihály Munkácsy's vast historical picture showing the Hungarians under Árpád receiving the

Statue of Ferenc Rákóczi II, with Parliament beyond

homage of the Slav tribes of the Carpathian Basin.

The Parliament in statistics

One thousand workers took 17 years to build the Parliament. It is 265m long, 123m wide and 96m high (the dome). It required 40 million bricks and 30,000 cubic metres of stone cladding, has 691 rooms, 17 gates, 29 staircases and 12 elevators. Only 23 years after completion, renovation had to begin (the stone chosen by Steindl was too soft).

Statuary around the Parliament

To the south is a statue of the 20th-century poet Attila József, seated overlooking the Danube he celebrated in verse. To the north is Mihály Károlyi, briefly prime minister of a democratic Hungary in 1918. On the square is the 18th-century freedom fighter, Ferenc

---

LAJOS KOSSUTH (1802–94)

A provincial lawyer and journalist, Kossuth made his first major political move by founding *Pesti Hírlap*, which (illegally) reported the proceedings of the Diet. He was briefly president of Hungary in 1848 but was forced into exile by the failure of the revolution. The rest of his life was spent abroad – in England, America and Italy, where he died. He remains a potent symbol of the Hungarian struggle for freedom.

Rákóczi II; and Lajos Kossuth to the north.

Kossuth Lajos tér. Group visits only to Parliament with tours or go to Entrance XII Wednesday to Sunday at 10am, in summer also at 2pm. Roosevelt tér 5. Tel: 268–4000.

PÁLYAUDVAROK
(Railway Stations)

Keleti Pályaudvar (Eastern Railway Station)

The second half of the 19th century saw the building of several iron and glass constructions in Budapest, chiefly market halls and railway stations inspired by English and French models. Budapest's Eastern Railway Station (designed by Gyula Rochlitz and János Feketeházi, 1884) has a 44m steel framework behind a rather grandiose neo-Renaissance façade. Two British engineers are honoured with statues high up on the triumphal arch that spans the main entrance: on the right is James Watt (1736–1819), inventor of the steam engine; on the left George Stephenson, (1781–1848) builder of the famous *Rocket* locomotive in 1829.

In the departure hall on the left are sententious murals by Károly Lotz and Mór Thán (badly in need of restoration). Despite the station's name, many trains from the west arrive here, just as trains for the north and east leave from the Western Railway Station.

The square in front of Keleti pályaudvar is named after Gábor Baross (1848–92), who was transport minister in the 1880s. He rationalised the Hungarian railway system by nationalising the six existing private railway companies. *Metro to Keleti pályaudvar.*

Nyugati Pályaudvar (Western Railway Station)

The first train on the first stretch of railway built in Hungary left for Vác on 15 July 1846 from the wooden predecessor to the present Western Railway Station. The architect responsible for this gracious example of industrial architecture (1877) was a Frenchman, August de Serres, and it was built by the famous Eiffel Company of Paris. In order to ensure that train services were not disrupted during construction work, the new station was built above and around the old one, which was demolished only when the work was complete.

The station has recently been restored, not quite authentically, since the (nonetheless attractive) blue paint on the ironwork is a post-modernist conceit. The former Royal Waiting Room, built for the arrival of Franz-Joseph and Elizabeth when they attended the Millennial celebrations of 1896, is in the east wing. Its ceiling features the coats of arms of the Hungarian counties served by trains from this station. To the right of the main entrance a sumptuous restaurant, redolent of the bourgeois comforts of the railway age, still stands ... now the most elegant McDonald's in Europe.
Teréz körút 109–111. Metro to Nyugati pályaudvar.

ROOSEVELT TÉR (Roosevelt Square)

The best surviving architectural feature of the square, which was once ringed by fine neo-classical buildings, is the Magyar Tudományos Akadémia (Academy of Sciences) at the northern end. After István Széchenyi offered a year's income from his estates for the founding of such an academy, the rest of the money for it was raised from public subscription. A plaque on the east wall (Akadémia utca) shows Széchenyi making his offer. When he was asked how he would live in the meantime, he explained dryly: 'My friends are going to support me.'

The Eastern Railway Station

The neo-Renaissance building was designed by a Berlin architect, Friedrich Stüler, and completed in 1861. Széchenyi's statue stands before it; on the plinth are figures of classical deities symbolising his multifarious achievements – Minerva, Neptune, Vulcan and Ceres (see page 82).

Also on the square are statues of Ferenc Deák (see page 79) and József Eötvös (1813–71), who reformed education in Hungary. The Jugendstil Gresham Palace (see page 57) stands next to the horrible 'Spinach Palace' (1979), while to the south is the no less horrible Forum Hotel, undoubtedly one of the worst architectural excrescences of the 1980s. Next to it is the less offensive Atrium Hyatt (1982). (See also pages 118–19.)

Bus 16 to Roosevelt tér. Tram 2 to Magyar Tudományos Akadémia.

Roman Remains

*I*n the first century AD the Romans planted a garrison in the Pannonian Celtic settlement of Ak-Ink ('Abundant Waters') and Latinised the name to *Aquincum*. An outpost across the Danube was known as *Contra-Aquincum* (see page 114). The military camp, on what is now Flórián tér (Óbuda), had its own baths and a huge amphitheatre with seating for 15,000. The civilian town was 2km to the north and there were other strategic *castra* and watchtowers, components of the famous defensive system along the Danube known as the *limes*.

Aquincum

The town originally existed to service the military – in every sense of the word. The brothels and pubs of the extensive rest and recreation area were collectively known as *canabae*. At the beginning of the 2nd century Trajan enhanced *Aquincum*'s status by making it the provincial capital of Pannonia Inferior. Hadrian raised it to a *municipium* in AD124 and in 194, under Septimius Severus, it became a *colonia*. The Roman governor (*legatus*) established his residence on the adjacent Óbuda island.

Aquincum flourished in the 2nd and 3rd centuries, partly due to its proximity

A surviving capital at *Aquincum*

to the amber trade route that ran from the Baltic through western Hungary to *Aquilea* on the Adriatic. Decline set in during the 4th century, at the end of which Rome was forced to make concessions to the Huns and withdraw from the area.

Sights of *Aquincum*

Substantial ruins of *Aquincum* remain, indicating the prosperity of a city numbering 40,000 inhabitants who enjoyed the benefits of an efficient water supply, sewage disposal and hypocaust heating. There were warm and cold baths and houses were decorated with frescos, mosaics and stucco. In the open-air part of the site are remnants of a

Ruins of *Aquincum*

ACCESS TO ROMAN REMAINS IN ÓBUDA

The general telephone number for the sites is 180–4650. Those that are accessible charge admission.

The **Amfiteátrum** (Military Amphitheatre), junction of Nagyszombat and Pacsirtamező utca (viewing from exterior only) – can be reached with buses 6, 84, 86 to Pacsirtamező utca.

Aquincum Museum, Szentendrei út 139; tel: 250–1650; open May to October, Tuesday to Sunday 10am–6pm; HÉV to Aquincum.

The **Cella Trichora** (viewing from exterior only), at the junction of Hunor and Raktár utca;

buses 6, 84, 86; tram 1 to Flórián tér.

Herkules Villa, Meggyfa utca 19–21; tel: 250–1650; open May to October by appointment only; buses 6, 86, 118, 142 to Bogdáni út.

Military Baths Museum, Flórián tér 3–5; tel: 250–1650; open May to August by appointment only; buses 6, 84, 86; tram 1 to Flórián tér.

Táborvárosi Múzeum (Roman Camp Museum), Aquincum; tel: 250–1650. See also page 110–11.

An excellent new publication in English is *Pannonia Hungaria Antiqua* (Archaeolingua)

forum, law courts, dwelling houses and religious (including Christian) sanctuaries. The museum contains everyday objects, either made locally or imported via the Rhine and the Danube from Germania and Gaul. Its star attraction is an organ worked by water pressure, a unique survival from Roman times.

Remains around *Aquincum*

South of the ruins is the so-called Herkules Villa, notable for mosaics depicting the labours of Hercules and Dionysian rites (wine production was encouraged in

Pannonia from the 3rd century). One vivid scene shows Hercules about to loose an arrow at a centaur abducting a curvaceous nymph.

Near by are the remains of a *cella trichora*, an early Christian chapel on a clover-leaf ground-plan. It dates to the 4th century and was probably built over a martyr's grave. Just to the north of *Aquincum* are the remains of an aqueduct and of the civil amphi-theatre, which is only half the size of the military one.

Roman column

Statues and Monuments

No free-standing monument from the Middle Ages has survived in Budapest, and most of those of the baroque age have been taken to the Kiscelli Museum in order to conserve them. The striking baroque Trinity Column (1713) on Szentháromság tér is an exception, but even this is largely a post-war replica. It is one of the classic Buda landmarks, on a spot where masses were held when plague epidemics closed the churches.

Today the visitor sees mainly 19th- and 20th-century statuary, the best of it nobly commemorating men worthy to be honoured, the worst of it (Socialist Realism) now mostly consigned to the new park of Communist monuments near Nagytétény (see pages 84–5).

Described below are monuments of historical and/or aesthetic interest. Many others are covered in the Walks (pages 102–23), or in the descriptions of Kossuth Lajos tér (see pages 72–3), Hősök tér (see pages 52–5) or Castle Hill and the Royal Palace (see pages 38–43).

Statue of Anonymous

ANONYMUS EMLÉKMŰ
(Anonymous Monument)
This is understandably the capital's best-loved monument (1903). The sculptor, Miklós Ligeti, was the beneficiary of money given by Emperor Wilhelm I of Germany, who visited Budapest in 1897 and remarked on the need for more statues in the city. He had in mind more bombastic representations of warriors, but the city authorities contented themselves with a few muscle-bound Turk-killers on Andrássy út. Ligeti's subject is very different. Master P was the anonymous monkish chronicler of Béla III, and his *Gesta Hungarorum*

St Gellért (Gerard Sagredo), first missionary to Hungary

(1204) was the first history of the Magyars. The sculptor has respected the historian's anonymity by hiding his face under his cowl.
Courtyard of Vajdahunyad Castle. Metro to Hősök tér.

BAJCSY-ZSILINSZKY EMLÉKMŰ (Bajcsy-Zsilinszky Monument)

The dramatic sculpture (by Sándor Győrfi, 1986) shows the politician who headed the non-Communist resistance to the Nazis at the moment of his arrest in Parliament by Hungarian fascists in 1944. He was shot shortly after his arrest. On the base of the monument is a quotation from Ferenc Kölcsey: '*A haza minden előtt*' ('the homeland before everything').
Deák Ferenc tér. Metro to Deák Ferenc tér.

DEÁK EMLÉKMŰ (Deák Monument)

Adolf Huszár's monument (1887) honours the lawyer and shrewd politician who was minister for justice in the independent government of 1848–49 and whose 'Easter Essay' in the *Pesti Napló* (16 April 1865) gave the impetus for the political Compromise of 1867 and the setting up of the Austro-Hungarian Dual Monarchy. Ferenc Deák was a man of outstanding integrity who lived for years as a bachelor in a suite of rooms in the nearby English Queen Hotel (the Gresham Palace was subsequently built on the site).
Roosevelt tér. Bus 16. Tram 2 to Roosevelt tér.

GELLÉRT EMLÉKMŰ (Gellért Monument)

On a dramatic site overlooking the Elizabeth Bridge rises the 6.76m bronze statue of Hungary's first missionary. Gyula Jankovics' work (1904) is supposedly situated near the spot where Gellért was either hurled to his death or rolled into the Danube nailed inside a barrel (versions differ). St Gellért (Gerard Sagredo) was born in Venice around 980 and martyred in 1046. He tutored King Stephen's son, Emeric, and was made Bishop of Csanád by King Stephen in 1030.
Buses 86, 5, 78 to Szarvas tér.

The symbol of freedom

KODÁLY ZOLTÁN SZOBOR
(Statue of Zoltán Kodály)
In a grove on the northeast slopes of Castle Hill is Imre Varga's remarkable bronze (1982) of the composer Zoltán Kodály (1882–1967), which has been likened to 'pop art'. Varga is a prolific creator of modern public monuments, highly naturalistic and often with a touch of humour.
Europapark. Várbusz from Moszkva tér to Bécsi kapu tér.

JÓZSEF NÁDOR EMLÉKMŰ
(Palatine Joseph Monument)
Johann Halbig's elegant bronze figure (1869), draped in the cloak of St Stephen's Order, honours the younger brother of Emperor Franz I. Archduke Joseph (1776–1847) headed the

Embellishment Commission (see page 96) that transformed the face of 19th-century Pest. He was one of the few Habsburgs to be loved by Hungarians.
Metro to Deák Ferenc tér, then a short walk to Nádor tér.

RAOUL WALLENBERG EMLÉKMŰ
(Raoul Wallenberg Monument)
Another bronze by Imre Varga (1987) is a belated tribute to the 'righteous Gentile' who saved thousands of Budapest Jews in 1944 by issuing them with Swedish identity cards. He probably died in the Russian *gulag* after the war.
Szilágyi Erzsébet fasor. Tram 56 (four stops) from Moszkva tér.

SEMMELWEIS SZOBOR
(Semmelweis Statue)
The marble statue (1906) of the 'Saviour of Mothers', Ignác Semmelweis (see also page 65), is by Alajos Stróbl. The sculptor depicted his own wife and baby as part of the ensemble in recognition of the fact that Semmelweis's improvements in medical practice had saved their lives after a difficult birth.
Rochus Hospital, Gyulai Pál utca. Metro to Blaha Lujza tér.

SZABADSÁG EMLÉKMŰ
(Freedom Monument)
As soon as the Russians had 'liberated' Budapest (and Vienna) they hastened to erect monuments in prominent places so that a grateful public should keep their contribution permanently in mind; the Freedom (formerly 'Liberation') Monument (1947) can be seen from most of Pest and much of Buda. Ironically Zsigmond Kisfaludy-Stróbl's work was originally intended to honour Admiral Horthy's son, a pilot killed in a crash thought to have been engineered by

the Germans. The addition of a Soviet soldier holding the red flag and one or two other touches adroitly made the iconographical switch from Horthyism to Communism. The massive female figure holding aloft a palm branch is still there, but the Soviet soldier has gone following the collapse of Communism.
Gellért-hegy. Bus 27 to Citadella.

SZOBORPARK (Sculpture Park)
The new home for the city's Communist statuary (see pages 84–5).
Balatoni/corner Szabadkai út (22nd District). Tel: 227–7446. Open: May to September, daily 8am–8pm; October to April, daily 10am–dusk. Admission charge. Yellow bus from stand 6 at Kosztolányi Dezső tér (about 20 minutes).

SYNAGOGUES

NAGYZSINAGÓGA (Great Synagogue)
The largest synagogue in Europe is still a centre of liberal Judaism. It was built by the Viennese architect Ludwig Förster (1859, enlarged 1931) in Moorish style, although the basilica-like ground plan and a cloister-like arcade are Christian in mood. Imre Varga's moving Monument to the Holocaust Victims in the rear courtyard recalls the terrible events of the mid-20th century and stands over the mass graves of victims. The attached Zsidó Múzeum (National Jewish Museum) is situated where the founder of Zionism (Theodor Herzl, 1860–1904) was born. It contains disturbing documentation of Jewish persecution.
Dohány utca 2–8. Tel: 342–8949 (museum), 342–1335 (synagogue). Synagogue open: March to October, Monday to Thursday 10am–2pm, Friday and Sunday 10am–1pm (except when there are ceremonies). Museum (Országos Zsidó Múzeum) open: Monday to Friday 10am–3pm; Sunday 10am–1pm. Corner Dohány utca/Wesselényi utca. Tel: 142–8949. Admission charge. Metro to Astoria.

ZSINAGÓGA (Orthodox Synagogue)
The rival to the liberal synagogue was the (moderately) orthodox one two streets away, which also has a vividly oriental look about it. The architect, Otto Wagner, was later to become the leading light of the Viennese Secession. Currently the synagogue is under restoration and difficult to visit.
Rumbach Sebestyén utca 11–13. Metro to Astoria.

Close by, in Dob utca, is a monument to the Swiss Karl Lutz, in the form of an angel stooping to help a fallen victim. Like Wallenberg, Lutz helped Jews to escape, although his method of buying their freedom remains controversial. For the synagogue in Óbuda, see page 111.

The Great Synagogue

Széchenyi Lánchíd
(Széchenyi Chain Bridge)

*I*n 1820 a 29-year-old nobleman was returning hurriedly from Bihar County to Transdanubia for the funeral of his father. He reached Pest on 29 December, only to find that the pontoon bridge over the Danube had been dismantled for three weeks. It was not until 5 January of 1821 that he could persuade a ferryman to negotiate the treacherous ice-floes. The nobleman was Count István Széchenyi and his reaction to this experience was to begin lobbying vigorously for the building of a long-mooted bridge between Pest and Buda.

On 10 February 1832, the Budapest Bridge Association was formed under Széchenyi's chairmanship. Following an old Central European tradition, it included not only enthusiasts, but also those who would otherwise have stymied the project out of jealousy, had they not been included. Opposition came from the municipalities, who were unwilling to forego the revenue of the pontoon toll, and from the nobility, who clung to their privilege of toll exemption which the owners of a privately built bridge were no longer prepared to indulge. However, the enlightened Palatine Joseph supported the project and the resistance of the aristocrats was finally overcome.

Széchenyi travelled to England to study bridge-building. He was impressed by William Tierney Clark's suspension bridge at Marlow in Buckinghamshire and Clark was invited to design the Budapest Bridge. A Scottish master-builder, Adam Clark (no relation), was engaged for the work. The project was jointly financed by Viennese bankers (Georg Sina, Samuel Wodianer and Jakob Rothschild). Construction (1842–48) was not without difficulties: as the last component was being lowered

---

COUNT ISTVÁN SZÉCHENYI (1791–1860)
Called 'the greatest Hungarian' by his political rival, Lajos Kossuth, Széchenyi was a reformer, a patriot and an enthusiast for technical innovation. He donated one year's income from his estates towards the foundation of the Academy of Sciences in 1827, and founded *inter alia* the National Theatre, the Danube Steamship Company, and the Óbuda shipyard. He also organised the regulation of the Danube and the Tisza, and improved the quality of Hungarian livestock, drawing on English expertise. Although he served briefly as transport minister in the independent government of 1848, his last days were clouded by mental instability. In 1860 he committed suicide in a Vienna sanatorium following harassment by the Habsburg police. His political and social attitudes may be summed up in his observation: 'We must struggle for the general good, as well as our own interest.'

into position, the chain of the hoist snapped, demolishing part of the scaffolding and pitching onlookers (including Széchenyi) into the Danube.

The Chain Bridge was completed just before the outbreak of the War of Independence and survived an attempt by the Austrians to blow it up. It was officially inaugurated after the war (by which time Széchenyi was confined to a Viennese mental asylum). Its imposing triumphal arches instantly became Budapest's most characteristic landmark, but the sculpted lions by János Marschalkó were criticised for apparently lacking tongues. The sculptor was able to demonstrate in several learned articles that lions' tongues 'do not hang out of the mouth like those of dogs'.

The city had given an undertaking to the construction company not to build a competing bridge either side of the Chain Bridge closer than a distance of 8km. Pressure of traffic soon made this condition intolerable and in 1870 the municipality bought the company out, so that construction of the Margaret Bridge could begin.

The Chain Bridge (above and below)

WHERE ARE THEY NOW?

The Communists stamped their presence all over Budapest in the form of street names and monuments, and newly elected city councils have been assiduous in removing these since the toppling of the regime in 1989.

Scores of names have been changed. Many were obvious candidates for oblivion – Engels Square or Lenin Avenue, for instance. Some were names associated with the obsessive Communist quest for legitimacy (Liberation Square, People's Army Square, First of May Avenue); others immortalised little-known minor functionaries.

In the autumn of 1992 work began on the removal (at huge cost) of 56 Communist statues from squares and parks, spurred on by activists of the Hungarian Association of Freedom Fighters of 1956. They announced that,

Statues of Communist heroes relegated to the Sculpture Park near Érd

if any were left *in situ* on 23 October (the anniversary of the 1956 revolution), they would tear them down with their own hands – a fate which befell the mega-statue of Stalin during the revolution itself.

Many of the Socialist Realist sculptures have been placed in a specially built park outside Budapest – a 'Disneyland of old Communism' as the deputy mayor described it. The presentation is dramatic: as you walk through a pedimented gateway flanked by over-lifesize statues of Lenin, Marx and Engels, a vista opens before you of heroically depicted groups of toiling workers or fighting soldiers, powerfully evoking the mixture of ideology and kitsch that passed for Communist art. In the view of the deputy mayor their preservation is itself an assertion of civilised values.

Meanwhile someone has discovered a warehouse full of Habsburg monuments that miraculously survived destruction in the 1950s. There are, of course, spaces for these now...
For location and details see page 81.

Váci utca, fashionable shopping mall

VÁCI UTCA (Vác Street)
Váci utca used to be two streets (it incorporated Lipót utca at the beginning of the 18th century) and they were quite different. However, the southern part, formerly decayed, has been transformed to resemble the pedestrian zone of the northern half. The latter has been likened to shopping malls such as Kärntner Strasse in Vienna or even London's Bond Street. It was always a

fashionable promenade, as 19th-century etchings show, but most of its fine neo-classical buildings have disappeared.

Number 9 is the Pest Theatre, built by József Hild in 1840 on the site of a famous hotel and ballroom where the 11-year-old prodigy, Franz Liszt, once gave a concert. Number 11a is faced with colourful Zsolnay ceramics and was built in the Jugendstil style by Ödön Lechner and Gyula Pártos (1890). Also worth a glance is the post-modern Tavern Hotel (no 20) by József Finta and Associates (1987), which is complemented by the same partnership's International Trade Centre opposite.

Váci utca seems to be awash with people night and day. There are Transylvanian ladies selling their fine embroidery, and stalls offering city guides, fragrance therapy, acacia honey and much else.
Metro to Ferenciek tere.

VÍGSZÍNHÁZ (Comedy Theatre)
The charming neo-rococo theatre was built by the Viennese firm of Fellner and Helmer. When it opened in 1896, the

FERENC MOLNÁR 1878–1952

Molnár made a career on Broadway as well as in his native Pest and is the best-known Hungarian dramatist abroad. His polished and witty comedies are full of psychological insight and erotic innuendo, transcending the milieu for which they were written. The Rodgers and Hammerstein musical *Carousel* was based on his play *Liliom* (1909), a low-life story set in the amusement arcade of the City Woodland Park in Pest. Asked how he became a writer, he replied: 'In the same way a woman becomes a prostitute. First I did it to please myself, then I did it to please my friends and finally I did it for money'.

The statue of Mihály Vörösmarty

public were sceptical of its chances of survival (it was too far out from the centre and had no funding from the state). In fact a diet of Hungarian and European comedies played in naturalistic style soon had audiences flocking to it. Ferenc Molnár was one who began his career here. Between the wars the staging of modern playwrights' work and visits by guest companies from abroad built up the theatre's reputation.
Szent István körút 14. Tel: 111–1650. Bus 6. Trams 4, 6 to Szent István körút. Renovation of the theatre is due for completion in 1994.

VÖRÖSMARTY TÉR
(Vörösmarty Square)

The spacious square is entered from Váci utca at a point where the inner city gate for the road to Vác (see page 134) once stood. Under the trees in the centre is a monument of Carrara marble (by Ede

Telcs and Ede Kallós, 1908) to the Romantic poet Mihály Vörösmarty (1800–55). The poet is shown reciting his *Szózat* (Appeal) to the Hungarian masses; etched on the plinth is a line from the poem: 'Be faithful to your land forever, O Hungarians!' Although *Szózat* contains more optimistic passages, the nightmare vision it evoked of '*nemzethalál*' (national extinction) spoke directly to the hearts of Hungarians, then as now.

On the north side of the square is a block built by József Hild, long known as the 'cutters' house' because a wealthy tailor, a surgeon, a slaughterer and a banker lived here (presumably the banker was seen as someone who could cut off the money supply). On the ground floor is the celebrated café and confectioner's, Gerbeaud (see page 170).
Metro to Deák Ferenc tér.

HUNGARIAN LIFESTYLE

For centuries Hungary was an agrarian feudal society, and many a city dweller is still provided by country cousins with home-made fare, vegetables and fruit. A popular 'rustic' tradition among young Budapestians today is the *szalonnasütés* (bacon barbecue). In a suitably rural environment, such as Szentendre Island, bacon is roasted with peppers and potatoes and Magyar folk songs are sung.

A more genuine peasant tradition is the December *disznóölés* (pig-killing); every part of the pig is used to make *kolbász* (sausage), *hurka* (black pudding), *sonka* (ham), *disznósajt* (pickled feet and ears), *kocsonya* (pork in aspic), *szalonna* (bacon) and *zsír* (lard).

While life in the country is still geared to the rhythm of the seasons, urban Hungarians often juggle their waking hours between two jobs in order to make ends meet. Life is hectic; by western standards it is also uncomfortable for most, due to a perennial shortage of accommodation. Young married couples are often condemned to live with in-laws, and most families have bedrooms that double as sitting-rooms. In the inner city, many live in hideous concrete 'panel-housing' blocks, notorious for tacky quality and lack of privacy. In the suburbs, life is more agreeable for those who live in family bungalows with lovingly tended vegetable gardens.

Suburbanites may keep fit by gardening, but city dwellers must turn to other means. Swimming in the spas is a popular pastime, combining as it does

The joys of eating, drinking and lazing

Street performers and
water chess

opportunities for gossip with
healthy exercise. At summer
weekends most of Budapest flees
to Lake Balaton, where many
people have built holiday homes.

More space, more cash and
more attention to diet are
beginning to have an impact on
Hungarian lifestyle. Unlikely to
change are the gregarious habits
of the Magyars, their capacity to
make much out of little, and their
ability to fill the calendar with
excuses for celebration. Every
day, it seems, is somebody's
name day, and therefore an excuse
for a visit that begins with the
enigmatic greeting: '*Isten éltessen
sokáig/a füled érjen bokáig*' ('May
God grant you a long life and may
your ears reach your ankles').

Várhegy
(Castle Hill)

*T*he wedge-shaped limestone plateau rising 160m on the west side of the Danube consists of the Royal Castle complex (see pages 38–43) at the southern end and the ancient town of Buda (the Várhegyed or Castle Quarter), encompassing the middle and northern parts of the plateau.

From the time of Béla IV in the 13th century, old Buda was a residential area ancillary to the court, where retainers, officials, craftsmen and merchants lived (see pages 26–7). Each component of its mixed population of Germans and Hungarians (also Walloons, Italians and Jews) has left traces here; even the last Turkish pasha has his monument, although there is very little else left to recall the 146-year-long Turkish rule. After the Diet ceased to meet in Buda at the beginning of the 19th century, Pest increasingly eclipsed Buda, until it gradually became the quiet backwater of today.

Access to Várhegy

Whether you want to visit the Royal Palace, the town, or both, the following access routes will apply: from the south the approach is on foot from Szarvas tér (reached by bus 86 on the Buda side, bus 78 from Pest) and brings you through the southern fortifications of the old castle. There are also various flights of steps up from Fő utca in the Víziváros (Water Town). The buses from Pest to Dísz tér on the southern end of the Castle Quarter are nos 16 from Erzsébet tér or 116 from Március 15 tér. The *sikló* (funicular) climbs from Clark Ádám tér at the west end of the Chain Bridge (daily 7.30am–10pm) and arrives at Szent György tér. The *várbusz* (minibus) runs between Szent György tér and Moszkva tér (metro red line) until mid-evening; it stops at strategic points in Buda town.

BÉCSI KAPU TÉR (Vienna Gate Square)

To the left of the gate are the lowering State Archives and opposite it is the Lutheran Church containing Bertalan Székely's picture, *Christ Blessing the Bread*. There are attractive baroque houses at nos 5 and 6, and the façade of no 7 is adorned with medallions of Virgil, Socrates, Quintillian, Cicero, Livy and Seneca.

The Crowning of King Stephen

DÍSZ TÉR (Parade Square)

The square is flanked by the Water Gate to the east and the Fehérvári or Jewish Gate to the west; to the south are the ruins of the War Ministry. Jews were settled close to the castle by Béla IV and held a Friday market here, until driven out by Louis of Anjou in 1360. Executions (a popular spectacle) were held on the square. In the middle is György Zala's *Honvéd Monument* (1893), honouring Hungarians who died for freedom in 1848–9.

FORTUNA UTCA (Fortuna Street)

French and Walloon craftsmen lived in the street in the Middle Ages. Gothic elements can be seen in several houses, notably the so-called *sedilia* (sitting niches) in the doorways (eg at no 5), a unique feature of Buda. They may have been used by traders for their wares or by servants waiting for their masters. At no 4 is the Museum of Commerce and Catering (see page 61).

Fishermen's Bastion (above)

HALÁSZBÁSTYA (Fishermen's Bastion)

Frigyes Schulek designed this neo-Romanesque viewing terrace to the east and south of the Mátyás-templom (Matthias Church); completed in 1905, it was named after the Danube fishermen who defended this bastion in the Middle Ages. The conical turrets are supposedly a romantic allusion to the tents of the original Magyar tribes. In front of the bastion is Alajos Stróbl's equestrian statue of St Stephen (1903) holding the (doubled) Apostolic Cross that symbolises his role as Christianiser of the Hungarians.

Attractive boutiques and a bookshop are to be found in the Fortuna Passage

HESS ANDRÁS TÉR (András Hess Square)

The square is named after the printer of the first Hungarian book (*Budai krónika – The Chronicle of Buda*, 1473) – his printing shop was at no 4. The Hilton Hotel (nos 1–2) is a modern adaptation of a former Dominican monastery and church. On the St Nicholas Tower of the former church is a copy of a 15th-century Saxon relief showing a triumphant King Matthias. Also on the square is the monument to Pope Innocent XI, initiator of the Holy Alliance formed to reconquer Buda from the Turks.

KAPISZTRÁN TÉR (Giovanni Capistrano Square)

Capistrano was a fiery Franciscan preacher who gathered an army against the Turks and took part in the successful

Church of St Mary Magdalene

siege of Belgrade in 1456. Appropriately the Museum of Military History is also on the square (nos 2–4, see page 60). On the Anjou Bastion beyond it is the monument to the last pasha of Buda, Abdurrahman Abdi Arnaut (actually an Albanian), who died at his post in 1686.

MAGDOLNA TEMPLOM (Church of St Mary Magdalene)

The tower and a solitary Gothic window of the choir are all that has been reconstructed after wartime bombard-ment of the church. It belonged to the Hungarians in the Middle Ages; after prolonged dispute a borderline between the German and Hungarian parishes had been drawn at the Dominican Monastery (now the Hilton) in 1390. Under the Turkish occupation the church was for a while shared between Protestants (worshipping in the nave) and Catholics (using the choir).
Kapisztrán tér.

MÁTYÁS-TEMPLOM (Matthias Church)

The Church of Our Lady is known as the Matthias Church after King Matthias Corvinus (1458–90), who considerably enlarged and enriched it. The interior was painted with polychrome geometric patterns and frescos in the 19th century by Károly Lotz and Bertalan Székely; the stained-glass windows show scenes from Hungarian history.

Against the north wall of the choir is the St Ladislas Chapel with a copy of the 14th-century silver bust of the 11th-century saint and king, Ladislas I, and frescos by Lotz illustrating legends about him. In the crypt are grave slabs of the Árpád dynasty. From there you begin a tour including St Stephen's Chapel, painted with scenes from the life of the

The Matthias Corvinus Church and one of
its stained-glass windows

saint-king, the Royal Oratory (containing
Habsburg coronation robes) and the
exhibition of ecclesiastical treasures in
the north gallery. Below it, in the Trinity
Chapel, is the tomb of Béla III and his
consort, Anne of Châtillon.
*Szentháromság tér 2. Tel: 355–5657.
Collection of ecclesiastical treasures and
religious art open 10am–6pm daily.*

HISTORY OF THE MATTHIAS CHURCH

The earliest church on this site dates
to the reign of Béla IV (1235–70). It
was enlarged in the late 14th century,
and subsequently Matthias Corvinus
built the oratory and replaced the
south tower that had collapsed in
1384. During the Turkish occupation it
was used as a mosque. Frigyes
Schulek entirely rebuilt it in neo-Gothic
style between 1874 and 1896, but
adhered to the original ground-plan.

The Church of Our Lady in the Middle
Ages was where the German burghers
of Buda held their services. The kings of
Hungary had to be formally accepted by
the community in the church following
their coronation in Székesfehérvár. After
the Compromise of 1867, Franz Joseph
and Elizabeth were crowned here, as
were the last Habsburgs, Karl IV and
Zita, in 1916.

Trinity Column and the neo-Gothic Central Archive

ORSZÁGHÁZ UTCA (The Street of the Diet)

The Italian craftsmen working on the Royal Palace once lived in this street (it was then called 'Olasz utca' – Italian Street). From the 1780s to 1807 the Hungarian Diet met at no 28, formerly a convent. Of the many attractive survivals, nos 18–22 retain Gothic and baroque features, while no 2 was a place of some splendour at the time of Sigismund of Luxembourg (note the sitting niches).

SÁNDOR-PALOTA (Sándor Palace)

Mihály Pollack and the Viennese Johann Aman designed this imposing neo-classical palace (1805–1821). It was the official lodging of the prime minister between 1867 and 1944 (see page 102). Note Anton Kirchmayer's frieze on the façade, a mixture of patriotic themes and scenes from antiquity. The building now houses the **Hungarian Historical Wax Works**.

Szent György tér 1–2. Open: 15 March to 31 October, 9am–6pm. Closed Monday. Guided tour in English available.

SZENTHÁROMSÁG TÉR (Trinity Square)

Trinity Square is the focus of the old town: to the east is the Matthias Church (see page 92), to the north the neo-Gothic Central Archive (formerly the Finance Ministry) and to the west the Régi budai városháza (Old Town Hall). This baroque fusion of five Gothic houses was seat of the council from 1710 to 1873. Szentháromság utca leads off to the west; at no 7 is the Biedermeier café Ruszwurm (see page 171). In the middle of the square is a Trinity Column (1713) commemorating the abatement of a plague epidemic.

TÁNCSICS MIHÁLY UTCA (Mihály Táncsics Street)

At no 7 is the baroque Erdődy Palace (1769) housing the Museum of the History of Music (see page 64). Number 9 may once have been the royal mint; it certainly became the Magna Curia (Royal Court) and was latterly a prison. The writer and agitator Mihály Táncsics was imprisoned here before the War of Independence. The Jewish ghetto was around nos 21 and 23. Number 26, formerly a synagogue, is now a museum. A wall plan shows the location of Buda's Jewish community at various periods. Dependent on the goodwill of the ruler, they suffered periodic persecution or expulsion. The Christian armies that reconquered Buda in 1686 massacred the Jewish inhabitants, who had established a *modus vivendi* with the Turks.

Synagogue museum, Tancsics utca 23 & 26 – tel: 155–8849. Open: 10am–2pm, weekends 10am–6pm. Closed: November to April.

Gates to the former Royal Palace

TÁRNOK UTCA (Treasurers' Street)

The name refers to the administrators of the royal monopolies (salt, minerals, etc) who resided in the area. The street was also the site of a market in the Middle Ages. Number 18 is a medieval building converted to a baroque apothecary's shop, now a museum with a display of utensils and period fittings.

Arany Sas Patikamúzeum – Golden Eagle Museum, Tárnok utca 18 – tel: 375–9772. Open: Tuesday to Sunday 10.30am–6pm.

ÚRI UTCA (The Street of the Lords)

At no 9 is the entrance to the cave labyrinth under Castle Hill (see page 136), while at the junction with Szentháromság utca is an equestrian statue of Maria Theresa's successful Hungarian general, András Hadik, who was also commandant of Buda for a while. His horse is a portrait of a famous stallion from the stud at Bábolna.

VÁRSZÍNHÁZ (Castle Theatre)

Originally a 13th-century Franciscan monastery, the building was occupied by the Turkish pashas between 1541 and 1686. It was turned into a German theatre in 1787 and saw the first ever Hungarian stage performance in the city on 25 October 1790.

Színház utca 5–9. Tel: 175–8011.

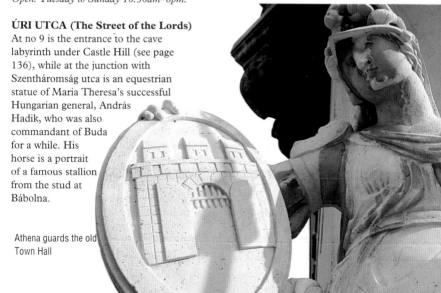
Athena guards the old Town Hall

Városliget
(City Woodland Park)

*T*he 1km-square Városliget is a playground for Budapestians, young and old, an historic landmark and a veritable paradise for lovers of trees with over 6,900 of them, including several rare species.

The area was once a hostile swamp through which meandered the stagnant waters of the Rákos Creek. In 1240 the Tatar army of Batu Khan inflicted a crushing defeat on the Magyars here by feigning a retreat and luring their opponents on to the marsh. In 1259 Béla IV granted what had now become pastureland known as the *ukur* (ox land) to the Dominicans of Margaret Island.

The sandy meadows were annexed to Pest by Leopold I, and Maria Theresa instigated systematic tree planting in 1751. The city's Embellishment Commission further improved the park, after holding a competition (won by a Bavarian landscape gardener, Henrik Nebbien) for the best ideas to beautify it.

The park contains several sights and museums covered on other pages: the Széchenyi baths (page 33), the Museum of Transport (page 61), the Agricultural Museum (page 61), the Amusement Park and the Zoo (page 155).

Chess in Városliget

THE EMBELLISHMENT COMMISSION

The popular Palatine Joseph threw his weight behind an imaginative 26-point plan for improving and beautifying Pest proposed by the architect János Hild. A commission set up to realise Hild's ideas first met in November 1808. Its primary business was urban planning to integrate the city core with fast developing new districts. It was regulations laid down by the Commission, concerning the maximum height of houses and their exterior decoration, that subsequently determined the unified aspect of neo-classical Pest. The Commission also gave its attention to the greening of the city through tree-planting and landscaping of Margaret Island and the City Woodland Park.

The ever-increasing financial burden it placed on citizens, who had to pay for the projects, contributed to the Commission's decline after 1830 and it was finally dissolved in 1856. In 1870 it was succeeded by the highly successful Council of Public Works, which planned the next and greatest phase of city expansion.

JÁNOS HUNYADI (c1407–56)
János Hunyadi was Hungary's greatest general in the early wars against the Turks, and the father of King Matthias Corvinus. He was Regent between 1446 and 1453.

Hunyadi rose to prominence at the court of King Sigismund, whose illegitimate son he was rumoured to be. His greatest triumph was at Nándorfehérvár (Belgrade) in 1456, a battle that stopped the Turkish advance for 70 years. Pope Calixtus III ordered the church bells of Christendom to be rung each day at noon in perpetuity to mark this victory.

VAJDAHUNYAD VÁRA
(Vajdahunyad Castle)
One of the most popular features of the 1896 Millennial Exhibition held in the City Woodland Park was Ignác Alpár's architectural phantasmagoria, originally a temporary structure, but by popular demand subsequently rebuilt in stone (1904–8). It presented a stylistic cross-section of architecture in Hungary through the ages. The Romanesque is represented by a replica of its best preserved example, the cathedral at Ják in western Hungary, and the baroque by the somewhat heavy neo-baroque of the Agricultural Museum. The *pièce de résistance*, however, is the Vajdahunyad Castle, which gave its name to the whole complex (its famous original was the seat of the Hunyadi clan in Transylvania – see box above). Additional Gothic and Renaissance sections copied from other buildings create a bizarre Hollywood effect, so that you half expect Errol Flynn to

Vajdahunyad Castle

jump out of a castle window. In the courtyard is Miklós Ligeti's fine statue of Béla III's chronicler (see page 78). The castle replica itself is one third of the size of the original in Romania.
Városliget is reached by metro to Hősök tere.

Views of the City

One of the joys of Budapest is that it can be viewed from so many different vantage points. Summer or winter, wind, rain, snow or sunshine, all create different moods and stress different aspects of the city.

VIEWS FROM BUDA
Várhegy (Castle Hill)

Castle Hill is ringed by bastions of which those on the northern and western sides have been turned into pleasant promenades. Views of the Vérmező (see page 49) and the residential quarter, Krisztinaváros, can be enjoyed from the chestnut-shaded Tóth Árpád sétány.

On the other side of the hill you can see the Parliament to best effect from Frigyes Schulek's Fishermen's Bastion

BUDAPEST ENVIRONS

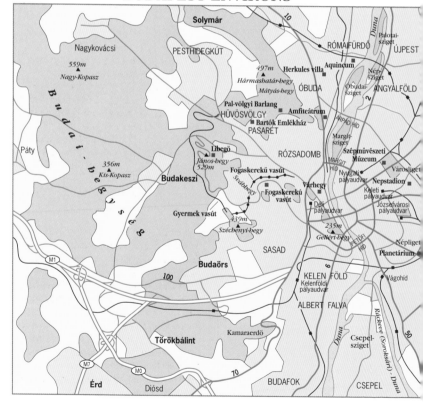

(see page 91). Further along the rim of Castle Hill to the south are excellent views from the terraces in front of the Castle Theatre and National Gallery. *Castle Hill districts can be reached with the várbusz from Moszkva tér.*

Budai-hegység (The Buda Hills)

The most fashionable area of Buda at the turn of the century was the Rózsadomb (Hill of Roses). Just beyond it is the now rather dilapidated look-out tower on József-hegy, with one of the best upstream views of the Danube (take bus 191 from Nyugati pályaudvar to the end stop). Further out is another tower, the vernacular Árpád-torony on Látó-hegy (bus 11 from Batthyány tér to end stop), one of the loveliest spots in the city.

The Hármashatár, Szabadság and Széchenyi hills all offer attractive vistas, but pride of place must go to the highest Buda hill, János-hegy (529m), which can be reached by bus 190 from Diana utca at weekends and holidays or with the chairlift from Zugliget. On the summit is the celebrated Erzsébet-torony (1910), named after Queen Elizabeth. Frigyes Schulek's tower has four levels of viewing platforms.

Gellért-hegy (Gellért Hill)

For dramatic views over the central and southern purlieus of the city and downstream Danube the best vantage points are from Gellért Hill, especially at night when the bridges are illuminated. From above, the Royal Castle to the north takes on a maquette-like character; below you the river surges toward the foot of the hill as if about to sweep it away.
Bus 27 from Móricz Zsigmond körtér to Citadella.

VIEWS FROM PEST

The fashionable Duna-korzó (the promenade between Chain Bridge and Elizabeth Bridge) offers the best panoramic views of the Royal Castle and Castle Hill. For a vista of Pest from an unusual angle, climb the cupola of St Stephen's Basilica (see page 46) – but be warned: there are over 300 steps! Finally, the 10th-floor Bellevue Restaurant of the Marriott Hotel offers a romantic (and gastronomic) experience for anyone who can afford it.

A CITY AND ITS RIVER

The Danube is the second longest river in Europe after the Volga: the Széchenyi Lánchíd (Chain Bridge) in Budapest is not yet half way along its 2,820km course. On the Budapest stretch it is generally around 5m deep, although there are some holes near Szabadság híd where it plunges to 8 or 9m.The bed is pebbles, loam and sand with outcrops of rock. The flood period is in June, and lowest water levels are reached in October and December.

In Roman times the river was the furthest boundary of the empire and, with its chain of fortresses (*limes*), a formidable barrier to threatening tribes from the east. Thereafter its greatest value was as a trade route – the 'dustless highway' in a chronicler's picturesque phrase. Goods had to be dragged upstream with teams of horses – or convicts where the bank was too treacherous for animals.

Things changed when the first steamship arrived in 1818. The journey from Pest to Vienna was cut from a month to three days and Hungarian agricultural exports boomed. The importance of Pest as a port was underlined by

the scale of Miklós Ybl's imposing Customs House (1874 – now the University of Economics); in the 20th century a free port was built on the edge of Csepel Island.

Until regulation in the 1870s, floods were a recurring hazard (there were 12 major ones between 1732 and 1838). To improve matters the main channel was made deeper and narrower and land was drained along the banks. Both the Parliament and the Technical University were built on reclaimed land. Floods are unlikely nowadays, but to

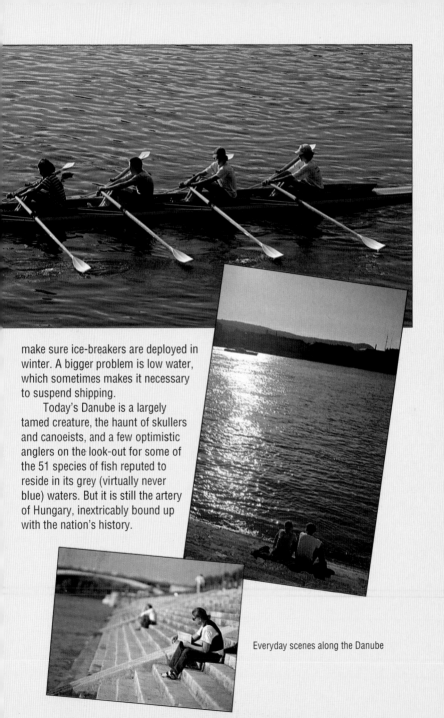

make sure ice-breakers are deployed in winter. A bigger problem is low water, which sometimes makes it necessary to suspend shipping.

Today's Danube is a largely tamed creature, the haunt of skullers and canoeists, and a few optimistic anglers on the look-out for some of the 51 species of fish reputed to reside in its grey (virtually never blue) waters. But it is still the artery of Hungary, inextricably bound up with the nation's history.

Everyday scenes along the Danube

Várhegy

This walk round Castle Hill gives a flavour of the old town of Buda, painstakingly restored after terrible destruction in World War II (see pages 90–5). *Allow 1½ hours.*

Start from the top of the funicular railway (sikló) that climbs to Castle Hill from Clark Ádám tér.

1 SÁNDOR-PALOTA (Sandor Palace)

On your right is the beautifully restored neo-classical former prime minister's residence (see page 94). A plaque on the east wall honours Count Teleki, head of the government in 1941, who committed suicide here when the decision was taken to

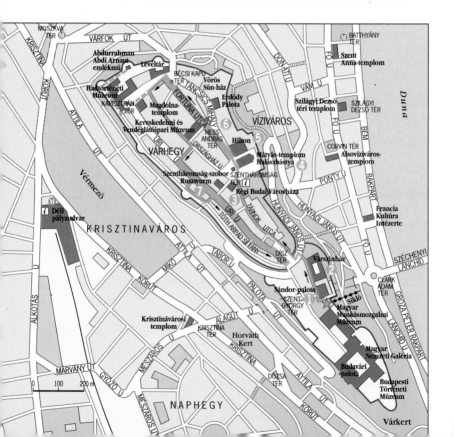

allow German troops through Hungary to attack Yugoslavia.

2 VÁRSZÍNHÁZ (Castle Theatre)

The former monastery was converted into a theatre (see page 95) by the engineer Farkas Kempelen, inventor of a 'speaking machine' and an 'automatic chess player' that once defeated Napoleon (it actually concealed a diminutive chess genius inside).

Walk through Dísz tér and Tárnok utca to Szentháromság tér.

3 RÉGI BUDAI VÁROSHÁZA (Former Town Hall of Buda)

The early 18th-century town hall on the west side of the square has a pretty bay window; below it is a statue of Pallas Athene, protectress of Buda. A clock tower with an onion dome rises from an upper-storey baroque chapel, dedicated to St John the Almsgiver (c 560–619).

4 MÁTYÁS-TEMPLOM, HALÁSZBÁSTYA (Matthias Church, Fishermen's Bastion)

The striking neo-Gothic reconstruction of the Matthias Church (see page 92) dominates the square's east side. If it looks a bit like a stage-set, the Fishermen's Bastion beyond it (by the same architect – see page 91) looks even more so.

5 HILTON HOTEL

Further north, the Hilton Hotel (1976) at Hess András tér 4 was ingeniously designed by Béla Pintér, incorporating the base of a medieval tower (now a casino), the remains of a Gothic church and a late baroque seminary.

A detour down Táncsics Mihály utca brings you past the Erdődy Palota (no 7) containing the Museum of the History of Music; next door (no 9) is where leading dissidents were imprisoned before the anti-Habsburg revolution of 1848.

6 HESS ANDRÁS TÉR/FORTUNA UTCA

At no 3 on the square is the ancient Vörös Sün-ház (House of the Red Hedgehog – see the relief above the door). Turn left at no 4 for the Litea bookshop/café and boutiques. Inside the baroque house at no 4 Fortuna utca is the Kereskedelmi és Vendéglatóipari Múzeum (Museum of Commerce and Catering – see page 61).

It is worth a detour on to the Anjou bastion to see the monument to the last Turkish pasha (Abdurrahman Abdi Arnaut emlékmű – see page 92). Walk back across Kapisztrán tér to Országház utca, leaving the stunted remains of the Magdolna-templom (Church of St Mary Magdalene on your right – see page 92). On the corner with Petermann bíró utca note the modern wall plaque of 'The Flying Nun'. It recalls the convent of the Poor Clares at Országház utca 28, later the seat of the Hungarian Diet.

Cut through Dárda utca and head south along Úri utca, where there are unusual Gothic sitting niches in the entrance to nos 31, 32 and 34. After catching the view over the Krisztinaváros from the west rampart (Tóth Árpád sétány), turn left by the equestrian statue to András Hadik (see page 95) into Szentháromság utca.

7 RUSZWURM

At no 7 is the famous confectioner's (see page 171). In the late 19th century, Vilmos Ruszwurm's pastries were in such demand that well-to-do Viennese ordered them to be sent by post-chaise.

Turn south out of the street for Dísz tér for buses to Pest, várbusz to Moszkva tér.

Rózsadomb and Víziváros

Elegant villas were built at the turn of the century on the Rózsadomb (Hill of Roses). The Víziváros (Water Town), so called for being constantly flooded, was settled by craftsmen and fishermen in the Middle Ages. *Allow 2½ hours.*

Start from the western end of the Margaret Bridge (Margit híd) and make your way to Frankel Leó út via Vidra utca.

1 LUKÁCS GYOGY-ÉS-STRANDFÜRDŐ AND MÁLOM-TÓ

At Frankel Leó út 25–7 is the Lukács spa (see page 33) with a

pleasant tree-shaded courtyard. On the wall are plaques erected by grateful beneficiaries of the healing waters. Across the street is a ruined Turkish gunpowder mill and a millpond (Málom-tó). If you walk through to the back of Lukács and turn left, you can see through a window the Turkish 'Császár Bath' built by Pasha Sokollu in 1570.
Turn up a cobbled street at the junction of Török utca and Frankel Leó út. Turn left before No 22.

2 GÜL BABA TÜRBÉJE

This tomb of a famous Dervish scholar (see page 50) is reputedly the northernmost Muslim shrine in Europe. It is customary to remove your shoes before entering.
Climb up to the junction of Gül Baba utca and Vérhalom utca. Make your way down Apostol utca to Rómer Flóris utca, across Margit körút and along Fekete Sas utca.

3 BEM SZOBOR (József Bem Monument)

The Polish general Bem fought for the Hungarians in the 1848 War of

Independence. The statue represents him urging on his troops. On the west side of the square are the offices of the Hungarian Democratic Forum.

4 FLÓRIÁN KÁPOLNA

The baroque chapel of St Florian (1760) is near by at Fő utca 90; peer through the glass entrance to see the frescoes and a finely carved pulpit. St Florian's has belonged to the Greek Catholics since 1920.

5 KIRÁLY GYÓGYFÜRDŐ

These baths (see pages 32–3) were built for the garrison under the Turkish occupation. In the dimly lit interior the play of light beams in the rising steam is an aesthetic experience. The baths are a centre of the Budapest gay scene.

6 ÖNTÖDEI MÚZEUM
(Foundry Museum)

A sign next to the baths points to this unusual museum. The exhibits deal with metal foundry from the Bronze Age to that of steel. Note the romantic statue of the engineer Abraham Ganz.

Continue south on Fő utca past the grim military prison (Nos 70–4), and the Nagy Imre tér.

Statue of General Bem

rococo inn 'At the Sign of the White Cross', behind which the post-chaise used to leave for Vienna. Szent-Anna templom (St Anne's Church – see page 46) is to the south. Next to it is the Angelika coffee house, sometimes described as the favourite rendezvous for the 'society of old hens'.

8 BATTHYÁNY TÉR TO CLARK ÁDÁM TÉR

Further along Fő utca is the Szilágyi Dezső teri templom (Calvinist Church) designed by Samu Pecz, whose statue stands beside it. Beyond it is the former Capuchin Church (No 32), remodelled in the 19th century. Opposite the neo-classical No 20 is the gracefully post-modern Francia Kultúra Intézete (French Institute – 1992).

Buses for Pest and Buda leave from Clark Ádám tér near by.

Öntödei múzeum
Bem József utca 20. Tel: 201–4370.
Open: Tuesday to Sunday, 9am–5pm.

---

7 BATTHYÁNY TÉR

The Szent Erzsébet-templom (Church of the Elizabethan Nuns) is on your left just before you reach the square. Their charitable tradition is maintained in the old people's home now occupying their convent. Immediately on the right is the

Tabán and Gellért-hegy

On this walk the self-confident architectural elegance of the 19th century is interspersed with glimpses of a turbulent past. *Allow 2 hours.*

Begin at Clark Ádám tér, reached by buses 16 from Pest or 86 along Fő utca on the Buda side.

1 CLARK ÁDÁM TÉR

The square, situated at the western end of the Széchenyi Lánchíd (Chain Bridge – see pages 82–3), is named after the bridge's Scots builder. Two fine blocks by Miklós Ybl

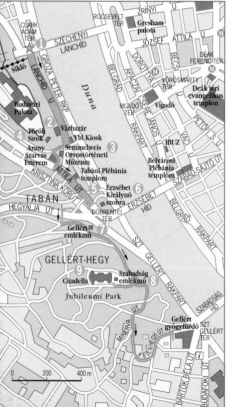

(1814–91) flank the northern side. To the west is the road tunnel under Castle Hill, also built by Clark. In front of the funicular railway (*sikló*) up to the castle is the modern kilometre stone, whence all distances from the capital are measured. *Walk 100m along the Lánchíd utca. On your right you come to the Várbazár.*

2 VÁRBAZÁR

This once elegant, now decayed, complex of steps and terraces was designed by Miklós Ybl to link the castle with the Danube shore. Across the street is a statue of Ybl in front of the 'Kiosk' (now a casino), which he built in neo-Renaissance style to camouflage the castle's water-pumping station.

3 SEMMELWEIS ORVOSTÖRTÉNETI MÚZEUM
(Semmelweis Museum of Medicine)

At Apród utca 1–3 is the neo-classical house of the Museum of Medicine (see page 65), named after the discoverer of puerperal fever, who was born here. József Antall, prime minister from 1990–3, was once director.

4 TÖRÖK SÍROK (Turkish Graves)

Steps lead upwards between the museum and another Ybl-designed house, where Adam Clark died. At the top follow the path round to the right. Under a locust tree are some lonely Turkish gravestones with inscriptions. *From here walk back southwards, passing the Arany Szarvas Étterem (The Golden Stag) restaurant in a simple baroque building on your right.*

5 TABÁNI PLÉBÁNIATEMPLOM (Tabán Parish Church)

The Tabán was a lively area of pubs and traders until its demolition in 1930. The parish church of St Catherine survives at Attila út 11. Many of the Tabán's inhabitants were Serbs, hence the name Rác fürdő (Serbian baths) of the establishment southwest of the church across the road junction.

6 ERZSÉBET KIRÁLYNÖ SZOBRA (Statue of Queen Elizabeth)

South of the church under the Elizabeth Bridge's feeder roads is the monument to Emperor Franz Joseph's wife, the pro-Hungarian Elizabeth of Bavaria. A plaque recalls that the previous monument on this site, to the pro-fascist politician Gyula Gömbös, was blown up by the Communist resistance in 1944. *Make your way under the spaghetti junction to the steps at the foot of the Gellért Hill.*

7 GELLÉRT EMLÉKMŰ (Gellért Monument)

A winding stairway leads to this memorial (see page 79) to the missionary St Gellért (Gerard of Csanád), allegedly martyred here.

Statue of Queen Elisabeth

8 SZABADSÁG EMLÉKMŰ (Freedom Monument)

The steep climb to the top of the hill is rewarded with stunning views. On the summit is the Freedom Monument (see page 80) put up at the end of the war by the Russians. The heroically represented Russian soldiers have been removed, leaving only an allegorical female figure.

9 CITADELLA (Citadel)

Above the monument is the ugly Citadella, built by the Austrians in 1854 as a barracks and fortress from which to control the unruly inhabitants of Budapest. It now has souvenir shops, a restaurant, a small hotel and a viewing terrace. *From here you can descend through a pleasant park to the Gellért spa (gyógy-fürdő) and the buses and trams on Gellért tér.*

Margitsziget

Margaret Island is Budapest's loveliest park with a history stretching back to Roman times. Originally it was three islands, the largest of which (Rabbit Island) was for long a royal hunting estate. 'Margaret' was the daughter of King Béla IV. She retreated to a convent here in 1252, when only nine years old. *Allow 1½ hours.*

The walk begins at the southern end of the island, reached with bus 26 from the east side of Margit hid (Margaret Bridge). Alight at the first stop on the island.

1 CENTENÁRIUMI EMLÉKMŰ (Centennial Monument)

The large fountain, colourfully lit at night, was erected in 1972. It commemorates the centenary of the unification of Buda, Pest and Óbuda in 1872–3.

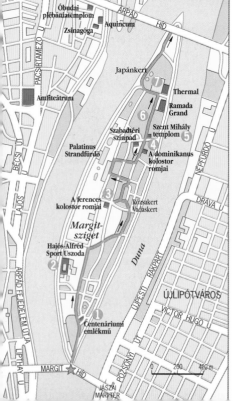

Open-air theatre on Margaret Island

2 HAJÓS-ALFRÉD SPORT USZODA AND PALATINUS STRANDFÜRDŐ

Serious swimmers can enjoy the massive indoor pool of the Hajós Baths, named after the gold medallist at the Athens (1896) Olympics. Hajós was also a successful architect and designed the pool and the building in 1930.

On the way to the Palatinus open-air baths (which have a mechanism for making artificial waves) you pass the attractive Rózsakert (Rose Garden) on your right.

3 FERENCES KOLOSTOR ROMJAI

Between the baths is a ruined Franciscan church dating from 1272. Palatine Joseph's splendid villa was built next to it in 1796 but destroyed in the 1838 flood. The Archduke encouraged development of the island's spa and laid out gardens, but the public were excluded until 1869.

4 DOMINIKÁNUS KOLOSTOR ROMJAI/SZABADTÉRI SZÍNPAD

Northeast of the Palatinus Baths are the ruins of the Dominican convent where St Margaret lived a life of daunting asceticism (even washing was viewed with suspicion). Not far to the west is a water tower and the open-air stage used for opera performances in summer.

5 SZENT MIHÁLY TEMPLOM (St Michael's Church)

To the northeast is the reconstructed Romanesque church of St Michael, built in 1930 using materials from the original 12th-century Premonstratensian church (ruins of the Premonstratensian convent are near by). In the church is a 15th-century bell, discovered in 1914 under a tree that had blown down in a storm.

St Michael's Church

The monks had probably buried it before the arrival of the Turks to prevent it being melted down to make cannons.

6 SCULPTURE AVENUE

Along the promenade to the Grand Hotel are busts of Hungary's greatest painters, poets and musicians. Among them is one of the 19th-century poet János Arany, who liked to sit under the island's trees in the evening composing his romantic lyrics.

7 RAMADA GRAND HOTEL, HOTEL THERMAL

Further north is the beautifully restored Grand Hotel designed by Miklós Ybl, a true reflection of a more leisured age. Beyond it is the ugly Hotel Thermal. To the west is the charming Japanese Garden.

At the northern end of the island, bus 26, which has a circular route, can be picked up again. Otherwise climb up to Árpád híd for buses to Óbuda or Pest.

Óbuda

High-rise blocks have ruined this once delightful area, but there are still a few pockets of historic interest and charm. *Allow 2 hours, 3 if the Kiscelli Múzeum is included.*

Take bus no 86 from Batthyány tér to Nagyszombat utca; or the HÉV railway to Tímár utca and walk back south.

1 AMFITEÁTRUM

This vast Roman arena was built for the military in the 2nd century and could accommodate 15,000 spectators. According to the medieval German epic *Das Nibelungenlied*, Attila the Hun ruled in the 5th century from 'Etzilburg', sometimes identified with this amphitheatre.

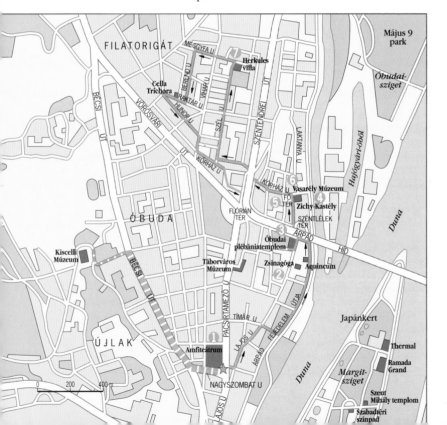

A longish detour via Nagyszombat utca and Bécsi út is required for the Kiscelli Museum (see page 61), housed in a former Trinitarian monastery on top of the hill.

Bear right along Lajos utca and right again along Timár utca. You emerge on a green sward bordered by Lajos utca and Árpád fejedelem útja.

2 ZSINAGÓGA

The fine neo-classical building of this former synagogue, at Lajos utca 163, was designed by András Landherr in 1825 for the growing Jewish community, many of whom were involved in the area's silk and leather-making industries. The synagogue is now a television studio; just beyond it is the new Hotel Aquincum, an especially pleasing brick and glass construction.

3 ÓBUDAI PLÉBÁNIATEMPLOM
(Óbuda Parish Church)

In front of the church (see page 45) is a lawn and chestnut avenue lined with sandstone statues. It stands on the site of the Roman military camp, part of which has been excavated. The tomb of Count Peter Zichy, who was given the lands of Óbuda by the king following the expulsion of the Turks, is beneath the pulpit inside the church. Just beyond is the Calvinist Church in Kálvin köz, notable for its presbytery (Károly Kós, 1909) in Transylvanian vernacular style.

Cross under Árpád Bridge to Szentlélek tér and Fő tér. In the passageway are the remains of the Roman military baths.

4 ZICHY-KASTÉLY (Zichy Mansion)

The baroque family home of the Zichys was built in 1757 by Henrik Jäger. It contains the Lajos Kassák Memorial

Rooms, dedicated to Hungary's greatest avant-garde artist and writer. Adjoining it is the Vasarely Museum with work by the founder of 'Op Art', Hungarian-born Viktor Vasarely.

5 FŐ TÉR

The delightful main square of Óbuda is flanked by baroque houses, several of them traditional Hungarian restaurants. At no 4 is an interesting collection of folk artefacts collected by Zsigmond Kun.

6 IMRE VARGA'S SCULPTURE

At the corner of Laktanya utca is *Strollers in the Rain*, Imre Varga's amusing sculpture of bronze ladies with umbrellas. More of his work may be seen at no 7.

Pass beneath Szentendrei út and bear right to the Herkules Villa.

7 HERKULES VILLA

The Herkules Villa, at Meggyfa utca 21, evidently belonged to a well-to-do Roman. From the same period are the remains of a rare *cella trichora* (clover-leaf chapel) at the junction of Hunor utca and Raktár utca. (See also page 77.)

Continue to Flórián tér where trams run to Pest or return to Szentlélek tér, for buses to Buda and Pest.

Zichy Mansion (Kassák Múzeum) – tel: 368–7021. Open: Tuesday to Sunday 10am–6pm.
Vasarely Museum – tel: 250–1523. Open: Tuesday to Sunday 10am–6pm.
Zsigmond Kun Collection (Lakasmúzeum) – tel: 250–0340. Open: Tuesday to Friday 2–6pm; Saturday and Sunday 10am–6pm.
Imre Varga Collection – tel: 250–0274. Open: Tuesday to Sunday 10am–17.30pm.

Szabadság híd to Ferenciek tere

This is one of two walks exploring the historic core of Pest. It begins just outside the former old city wall. *Allow about an hour.*

Start at the Pest side of Szabadság híd (see page 37).

1 KÖZGAZDASÁGTUDOMÁNYI EGYETEM
(University of Economics)

The former 'Karl Marx University' at Fővám tér 8 was one of the more liberal institutions under Communism. The noble building is one of Miklós Ybl's finest works (1874) and was originally the Customs House. Its grandeur and size (170m

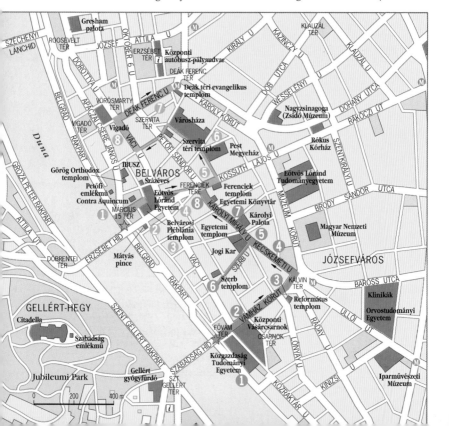

long, 56m deep) reflect Pest's importance as a centre of Danubian trade in the late 19th century.

2 KÖZPONTI VÁSÁRCSARNOK (Central Market)

Behind the university is the largest of Pest's five market halls, opened in 1897 as a spin-off from the 1896 Millennial Celebrations (see page 145).
Walk east along Vámház körút as far as Kálvin tér.

3 REFORMÁTUS TEMPLOM (Calvinist Church)

This rather plain neo-classical church (see page 46) took 14 years to build in the early 19th century due to funding problems. It achieved its present form in 1859. Inside is the tomb of Countess Zichy (who was Anglican by faith). The Calvinist College at nearby Ráday utca 28 has an interesting display of bibles (enquire at the entrance).
From Kálvin tér it is a few minutes' walk on Múzeum körút to the Magyar Nemzeti Múzeum (Hungarian National Museum – see pages 62–3). Otherwise turn left into Kecskeméti utca.

4 THE OLD CITY WALL

The post-modern Hotel Korona, with a bridge section over-arching the road, stands on the site of the city gate. Just beyond the archway is an inscription on the wall: '*Itt állt a középkori pesti városfal*' ('Here stood the medieval city wall of Pest').

5 JOGI KAR AND EGYETEMI TEMPLOM (Faculty of Law and University Church)

Further along the street on your left is the elegant neo-baroque Faculty of Law and adjoining it the University Church

(1742), probably the work of Andreas Mayerhoffer (see page 44). In the early 19th century it was a centre of the reform movement. A school for nurturing and promoting the Hungarian language (in opposition to German) was founded here in 1831.
Turn left down Szerb utca.

6 SZERB TEMPLOM (Serbian Church)

You now come to the pretty Serbian Church (see page 47) built by the Serbian community in 1698. It is said that at the beginning of the 19th century every fourth house in Pest was owned by a Serb merchant.
Retrace your steps to Károlyi Mihály utca.

7 KÁROLYI-PALOTA (Károlyi Palace)

Károlyi Mihály utca 16 was the city residence of Count Mihály Károlyi, first president of the Hungarian Republic in 1918. His widow, known as the 'red countess', kept an apartment here towards the end of her life. Mayerhoffer's baroque palace was given its neo-classical aspect in 1799.

8 EGYETEMI KÖNYVTÁR (University Library)

At the end of Károlyi Mihály utca is the south side of Ferenciek tere (Square of the Franciscans). At no 10 is the freshly restored University Library, an impressive neo-Renaissance building (1876). There are frescos in the reading room by Károly Lotz and Mór Than. Eleven codices from the great library of King Matthias Corvinus are kept here.
Buses leave from Ferenciek tere for various destinations and there is also a metro stop for the blue line.

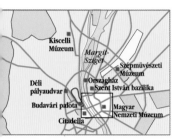

Erzsébet híd to Deák Ferenc tér

The walk begins at the Roman fort where Pest originated, and includes the fashionable shopping area of Váci utca. See map on page 112 for route. *Allow 1 hour.*

Start in front of the church at Március 15 tér at the Pest end of Erzsébet híd (see page 37).

1 CONTRA AQUINCUM

This diminutive fortress (see page 76), with walls 3m thick, was a 4th-century outpost in barbarian territory protecting the main town of Aquincum on the far side of the river.

2 MÁTYÁS PINCE

If you want to experience a typical (if touristified) Hungarian restaurant with gypsy music, cross under the bridge to the Mátyás pince at Március 15 tér 7, an institution since it opened in 1904.

3 BELVÁROSI PLÉBÁNIA-TEMPLOM (Inner City Parish Church)

The most historic church of Pest (see page 44) is on Március 15 tér. It has had an eventful history: the Romanesque and Gothic churches were both largely destroyed, while the Turks turned the diminished building into a mosque. Highlights of the mostly baroque interior are the two lovely Renaissance tabernacles made of red marble.

A detour to the north takes you to the Görög Orthodox templom (Greek

Vörösmarty statue

Orthodox Church) at Petőfi tér 2 (drop in to hear the singing at 6pm on Saturdays).

4 EÖTVÖS LÓRÁND EGYETEM
(Lóránd Eötvös University)
Named after the distinguished physicist (1848–1919), Budapest's main university was originally a Piarist 'gymnasium' (secondary school). You pass under the building's connecting archway on your way to Kigyó utca and thence to Ferenciek tere. In the parallel Pesti Barnabás utca, at No 2, is the Százéves (100 Years) restaurant, located in one of the few remaining baroque palaces of Pest.

5 PÁRIZSI UDVAR (Paris Arcade)
Flanking Ferenciek tere to the north is the striking Jugendstil arcade designed by Henrik Schmahl (1911), with its oriental-looking stained-glass cupola. There is a good bookshop here, a newsagent with foreign newspapers and the popular Piccolo bar. Across Kossuth Lajos utca is the Ferenciek templom (Franciscan Church – see page 45). On the north wall is a relief showing Count Wesselényi rescuing Pest inhabitants by boat during the floods of 1838.
Now take the next street to the left after Petőfi Sándor utca.

6 PEST MEGYEHÁZA, VÁROSHÁZA (County and City Halls)
The Pest County Hall (No 7 Városház utca) is a simple neo-classical building (1830), while the City Hall (Nos 9–11) is an elegant baroque work (Antonio Martinelli, 1735), originally a hospital for war wounded, established by Emperor Charles VI. An imposing

Atlas bearing a globe stands over the entrance.

7 SZERVITA TÉR (Servite Square)
The street leads to the square recently renamed after the Servite Order, whose church (1725) stands on the corner (see page 47). Two fine Jugendstil houses (see page 57) at Nos 3 and 5 are worth a glance, especially the mosaic in the gable of No 3, a florid representation of 'The Transfiguration of Hungary'.
Turn left into Petőfi Sándor utca and immediately right into Régiposta utca; then right into Váci utca.

Váci utca bookshop

8 VÁCI UTCA TO VÖRÖSMARTY TÉR/GERBEAUD CUKRÁSZDA (Coffee House)
This fashionable shopping area (a pedestrian zone) is always thronged with people. On the square is the monument to the poet Mihály Vörösmarty (1800–55). At the north end is the celebrated 1870 Gerbeaud coffee house and confectioner's, with its enticing menu of Viennese and Hungarian pastries (see page 170).
The metro junction, where the three lines meet, is at nearby Deák Ferenc tér to the east.

HUNGARIAN FOLK ARTS

Hungary's folk traditions have long reflected diverse ethnic groups (Ruthenians, Slavonians, Slovaks, Rumanians and Serbs as well as Magyars). Despite commercialisation, beautiful handicrafts are still produced, and the charm of folk song and dance is undimmed. Surviving peasant architecture provides a fascinating insight into a way of life not totally extinct.

Budapest visitors may first glimpse folk embroidery as they pass the Transylvanian women who sell their wares at the entrance to the metro or on Castle Hill. Their speciality is the lovely red (or sometimes blue) 'tulip' or 'heart' pattern on a white background. Other regions produce delicate open

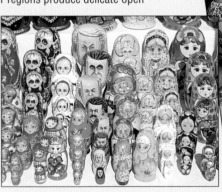

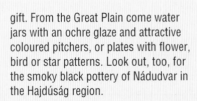

work, wool embroidered cushion ends and beautifully ornamented aprons, tablecloths or handkerchiefs. Dense multi-coloured needlework for folk costumes is a Matyó speciality from northern Hungary.

Pottery is a traditional wedding gift. From the Great Plain come water jars with an ochre glaze and attractive coloured pitchers, or plates with flower, bird or star patterns. Look out, too, for the smoky black pottery of Nádudvar in the Hajdúság region.

The horsemen, shepherds and swineherds of the Great Plain specialise in carved artefacts, such as whip handles, crooks, axes, mirror frames or tobacco boxes. Look out for beautiful folk carving if you visit the Protestant churches of Southern Transdanubia and the Upper Tisza.

The place to see peasant architecture is a *skanzen* (an open-air museum village such as the one at Szentendre, see page 133). The houses often had wattle-and-daub walls and roofs thatched with reeds.

Folk entertainments – dancing, singing and seasonal celebrations – may be seen all over Hungary, but especially at Hollókő in the north, home of the Palóc people. Eastertime here harks back to pagan purification and fertility rites. The girls paint beautiful floral designs on eggs and must run the gauntlet of young men sprinkling them with well water.

Hungarian folk culture includes music, dancing, pottery and textiles

A colourful brochure of folklore events and performances is obtainable from Tourinform, Sütő utca 2, tel: 117–9800, fax: 117–9578.

Deák Ferenc tér to Kossuth Lajos tér

The walk explores the institutional quarter of Pest.
Allow 2 hours.

Begin at Deák Ferenc tér and walk northwest across
Erzsébet tér, leaving the international bus station on your right. On
your left you will see the new Corvinus Kempinski Hotel, and on the
corner of Harmincad utca the huge former bank occupied by the
British Embassy.

1 DANUBIUS-KÚT (Danubius Fountain)

In the middle of Erzsébet tér is this triple-basined fountain, a
copy of Miklós Ybl's beautiful original.
The ladies perched on the lower bowl
represent Danube tributaries – the Tisza,
Dráva and Száva.
Go through the passageway between the
buildings on Bécsi utca to the south.

2 JÓZSEF NÁDOR EMLÉKMŰ

Johann Halbig's statue of Palatine Joseph
of Hungary stands in the square. The
sixth son of Emperor Leopold II, the
Archduke was Palatine of Hungary from
1796 until his death 50 years later. He did
much to realise Hungarian aspirations
and moderate the policies of the
Habsburg court in Vienna.
Turn left down József Attila utca and right
into Roosevelt tér.

3 ROOSEVELT TÉR

The square (see pages 74–5) is flanked by
the Forum and Atrium Hyatt hotels at the
southern end and the elegant Magyar
Tudományos Akadémia (Academy of
Sciences) to the north. There are statues
of 19th-century statesmen – József Eötvös
(who reformed public education), Ferenc
Deák (who organised the 1867

Compromise with the Habsburgs) and István Széchenyi (see page 82). On the east side are the Ministry of the Interior, the Jugendstil Gresham Palota (Palace) and an office block known as the 'Spinach Palace', because of its colour. *Walk along Akadémia utca and turn right down Széchenyi utca, which leads to Szabadság tér.*

4 SZABADSÁG TÉR
The former stock exchange on the west side is now the TV Székház (Hungarian Television Centre); opposite is Ignác Alpár's eclectic Nemzeti Bank (National Bank – 1905). North of that is the Jugendstil American Embassy, where Cardinal Mindszenty took refuge during the 1956 revolution – and remained for 19 years. The statue near by is of an American general who prevented Romanian troops from looting the National Museum in 1919. Ödön Lechner's marvellous Postatakarék-pénztar (Post Office Savings Bank – see page 59) is round the corner (Hold utca 4). Just to the north is the Batthyány-örökmécses (Eternal Flame) commemorating the 13 Hungarian generals executed by the Habsburgs in 1849. The prime minister of the independent government, Count Lajos Batthyány, was shot on this spot. *Walk on to Hold utca and turn left into Alkotmány utca, which leads to Kossuth Lajos tér.*

5 KOSSUTH LAJOS TÉR
This vast space is dominated by Imre Steindl's Országház (Parliament – see pages 72–3), the most ambitious construction project ever undertaken in Hungary. From 1885 some 1,000 labourers and craftsmen worked on it for 17 years. The vast red star of the

The Eternal Flame

Communist era was removed from the spire after 1989 at considerable cost.

Alajos Hauszmann's Supreme Court (Kossuth Lajos tér 12), now the Neprajzi Múzeum (Ethnographical Museum), and the Mezögazdasági es Elelmézesügyi Min. (Ministry of Agriculture) occupy the southeast side. The heroic statues on the square represent Lajos Kossuth and Ferenc Rákóczi II, 19th- and 18th-century heroes, respectively, of the struggle for independence. *Walk up past the 'White House', formerly the sinister headquarters of the Communists, now offices for Parliamentarians. Tram and bus stops are at the Pest end of Margit híd.*

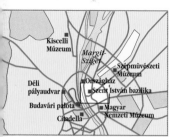

Andrássy út

This walk takes you along the grandest boulevard
of Pest, with a diversion through theatreland.
Allow 1½ hours.

*Walk from the metro stop at Deák Ferenc tér across the
east side of Erzsébet tér to the corner of Bajcsy-Zsilinszky
út and József Attila utca.*

1 INTERNATIONAL TRADE CENTRE
Fans of post-modern architecture will appreciate the reflecting
glass and futuristic sculpture of this building (Bajcsy-Zsilinszky
út 12) by József Finta and associates. Finta's work is
everywhere – he landed many of the plum contracts for hotels
in the Communist period, including the Intercontinental, the
Forum and the Taverna.
*A short detour down Bajcsy-Zsilinszky út brings you to St Stephen's
Basilica (see pages 46–7). Otherwise bear diagonally to the right.*

2 ANDRÁSSY ÚT
Originally called Sugár (Radial) út, the boulevard has reflected
political events in its many name-changes. It was named
Andrássy in 1885 after the distinguished prime minister and
foreign minister (1823–90). Under Communism it was first
called Stalin Avenue, then briefly Avenue of Hungarian Youth

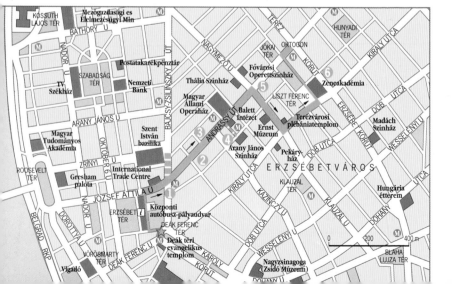

(during the 1956 revolution), then Avenue of the People's Republic, and now once again Andrássy út.

3 MAGYAR ÁLLAMI OPERAHÁZ
(Hungarian State Opera)
This is one of Miklós Ybl's most opulent public buildings (see pages 66–7). Emperor Franz Joseph financed it and attended the opening on 27 September, 1884, when Ferenc Erkel's national opera *Bánk Bán* was performed.
Opposite the opera is an early building by Ödön Lechner (see pages 58–9), now used by the corps de ballet. Go down the street beside it (Dalszínház utca) to Új Színház.

4 ÚJ SZÍNHÁZ
(New theatre)
This beautifully restored art deco theatre at Paulay Ede utca 35 is worth a visit simply to marvel at the interior (new, but done entirely in the spirit of the original).

5 NAGYMEZŐ UTCA
Further east on Andrássy út you come to Nagymező utca, once the Broadway of Budapest, and still boasting several theatres. Turn right down it; at no 8 is the revived Ernst Múzeum, containing modern Hungarian and foreign art. The Jugendstil house was partly designed by Ödön Lechner and the stained-glass window of the staircase is by József Rippl-Rónai (tel: 341–4355; open: Tuesday to Sunday 10am–6pm). Continue down Nagymező utca to the junction with Király utca, where you will see the late baroque Terézváros Parish Church (1809). The open gangway running round the tower was the fire-watch. Inside are two fine neo-classical altars designed by Mihály Pollack (who built the National Museum). Across the junction at Király utca 47 is the

Statue of Bajcsy-Zsilinszky

extravagantly romantic Pékary-ház (National Savings Bank). Note the statues of fierce Magyar chieftains over the portals.
Turn left along Király utca until you reach the southern end of Liszt Ferenc tér.

6 ZENEAKADÉMIA
(Music Academy)
The Music Academy (1907) at Liszt Ferenc tér 8 (see pages 68–9) is a bizarre mixture of Hungarian national style and eclectic features. Most striking is the gilded and ceramic-clad foyer. Symphonic, chamber and choral works are given in the auditorium, which is famous for its good acoustics.
Walk north through the square, passing the controversial modern statue of Franz Liszt (László Marton, 1986) and (at the Andrássy end) a statue of the poet Endre Ady, scourge of corrupt Magyar society at the turn of the century. Turn right on Andrássy út for the metro at Oktogon.

Oktogon to Gundel Étterem

This walk is mostly concerned with the legacy of the Millennial Celebrations of 1896, held 1,000 years after the Hungarians first entered the Carpathian Basin. *Allow 2 hours.*

Start from the metro station (yellow line) at Oktogon and walk east along Andrássy út.

1 FORMER ÁVH HEADQUARTERS – ANDRÁSSY ÚT 60

The ÁVH, the secret police of the Communist regime, had their headquarters in this building, which they took over from their Nazi counterparts. A plaque on the wall recalls that Cardinal Mindszenty was tortured here. The policeman responsible recently died, uncharged, at a ripe old age.

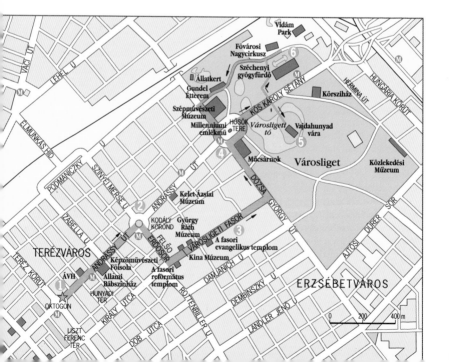

2 KODÁLY KÖRÖND

The roundabout is named after the composer Zoltán Kodály, whose Memorial Museum is at no 1. At each corner of the roundabout are statues of Hungarian heroes of the Turkish wars. *Turn right down Felső erdősor utca and left into Városligeti fasor.*

3 VÁROSLIGETI FASOR

At Városligeti fasor 5–7 is Aladar Árkay's curious Fasori református templom (Calvinist Church – 1913), combining Hungarian vernacular with Finnish influence. Over the porch are tiles decorated with Magyar folk motifs, which recur in the impressive interior. No less remarkable, at Városligeti fasor 17, is Samu Pecz's neo-Gothic Fasori evangelikus templom (Lutheran Church – 1905). Gyula Benczúr painted the *Adoration of the Magi* on the high altar. At no 12 is the György Ráth Múzeum, containing Chinese and Japanese artefacts. All along the tree-lined avenue are elegant turn-of-the-century villas, one of which belonged to the well-to-do family of the Marxist philosopher, György Lukács.

You can rejoin Andrássy út via Bajza utca or walk down to Dózsa György út and turn left, passing the area where the Communists held their propaganda rallies.

4 HŐSÖK TERE (Heroes' Square)

The square (see pages 52–3) is a national focus of identity created for the Millennial Celebrations. On your right is the Műcsarnok, an exhibition hall devoted to modern art; on your left is the Szépművészeti Múzeum (Museum of Fine Arts – see page 65).

The column in the centre of the square is topped by the figure of the Archangel Gabriel who, according to one legend, was responsible for suggesting to Pope Sylvester that he send a crown to King Stephen in AD 1000 (see page 8). Round the base are mounted Magyar chieftains. Kings and national heroes are displayed in the pantheon at the rear. *Beyond Heroes' Square cross the Városligeti tó (lake) on the Kós Károly sétány and turn right down the Vajdahunyad sétány. Rowboats are available on the lake in summer and in winter it becomes an ice rink.*

5 VAJDAHUNYAD VÁRA
(Castle of Vajdahunyad)

Ignác Alpár's architectural fantasy on the artificial island (see page 97) boasts a replica of Vajdahunyad Castle in Transylvania. Other features include a replica of the Romanesque cathedral at Ják (Western Hungary), the Agricultural Museum and the statue of King Béla III's anonymous chronicler.

6 SZÉCHENYI GYÓGYFÜRDŐ/ ZOO/GUNDEL ÉTTEREM

A stroll back across the Városliget brings you to the Széchenyi Baths (see page 33), the zoo (Állatkert), Vidám Park (amusement park – see page 155) and the celebrated Gundel Étterem (Restaurant) at Állatkerti út 2, now restored to its turn-of-the-century splendour by George Lang. *The metro (yellow line) leaves from Hősök tere.*

Kodály Memorial Museum – tel: 342–8448. Open: Wednesday 10am–4pm, Thursday to Saturday 10am–6pm, Sunday 10am–2pm. **György Ráth Museum** – tel: 342–3916. Open: Tuesday to Sunday 10am–5.45pm.

Excursions

LAKE BALATON

One hundred kilometres southwest of Budapest is Lake Balaton, Central Europe's largest inland sea with a shoreline of 200km, a surface area of 595sq km and an average depth of no more than 2m. Its warm waters (30°C in summer) make it Hungary's most popular resort. Sailing, windsurfing and horse-riding are additional attractions, as is fishing: there are 40 different species of fish in the lake, the most famous being the indigenous *fogas* (pike-perch).

TIHANY

The Benedictine abbey of Tihany is situated on a basalt promontory overhanging the deepest part of the lake. It was founded by Andrew I in 1055 and its baroque church contains beautiful carving by Sebestyén Stulhoff. The ample-bosomed angel on the Altar of the Virgin Mary is supposed to be a portrait of the artist's beloved, a local fisherman's daughter. The Romanesque crypt contains the simple gravestone of King Andrew, who died in 1060.

Other sights of interest include the Tihany Museum, in the former priory. The display covers local topography and the origins of the Magyars; one room is devoted to the physicist Lóránd Eötvös (1849–1919), who conducted experiments on the Balaton ice-pack. The rustically furnished House of the Fishermen's Guild, off Pinsky Promenade, has material on the life of the Balaton fishermen. To the north is the Visszhangdomb (Echo Hill) and beyond that the Óvar (Old Castle ruin). In its rock base Orthodox monks carved out their hermit cells.

BADACSONY

A little further west is the table-top volcanic mountain of Badacsony. Its vine-clad slopes produce some of the region's best wines, notably *Szürkebarát* (Pinot Gris). The southeastern face has impressive basalt columns over 50m high. In the town centre, just north of the main road, is the József Egry Memorial Museum, devoted to the Balaton's famous local painters.

The delightful country house of Keszthely

Balaton Museum – Múzeum utca 2, Keszthely. Tel: 06/83/312351. Open: Tuesday to Sunday 10am–6pm (October to April, Tuesday to Saturday 9am–5pm).
Beszédes József Museum – Sió utca 2, Siófok. Tel: 06/84/311071. Open: Tuesday to Sunday 9am–1pm, 2–6pm.
Festetics country mansion – Kastély utca 1, Keszthely. Tel: 06/83/312191. Open: daily 10am–5pm.
József Egry Memorial Museum – Egry sétány 12, Badacsony. Tel: 06/87/431140. Open: 1 May to 31 October, Tuesday to Sunday 10am–6pm.
Tihany Museum – Batthyány utca 36. Tel: 06/87/448650. Open: May to September, Tuesday to Sunday 10am–5pm.

Vines at Badacsony

KESZTHELY

At the lake's western end is the town of Keszthely with the Festetics country mansion. Count György Festetics (1755–1819) lived here in 'retirement' (semi-exile) after taking part in a failed rebellion against the Habsburgs. While here he founded the Helikon circle of reform-minded intellectuals and an agricultural university known as the Georgikon. The high point of the tour of the interior is the Helikon Library, beautifully constructed from Slavonian oak by a local carpenter.

In the town the Balaton Museum covers zoological, ethnological and archaeological aspects of the region.

OTHER PLACES OF INTEREST

At the lake's east end the spa of Balatonfüred has charm. Hévíz (8km from Keszthely) is a thermal lake fed by a source 1km below the surface (the baths are open 7am–4pm). The marshy Kis-Balaton at the lake's western tip, where the River Zala runs into it, is good territory for birdwatchers. Along the southern shore there are many resorts, of which Siófok is the biggest and ugliest. However, its Beszédes József Museum is worth seeing for the history of the nearby Sió canal that connects Lake Balaton with the Danube.

Lake Balaton is 100km southwest of Budapest. Trains leave from Déli pályaudvar (Southern Railway Station).

Local handicrafts on show

The view from Visegrád

DUNAKANYAR
(The Danube Bend)

The Danube enters Hungary flowing west to east, but after Esztergom it is forced into an S-shape in a narrow valley between the Pilis and Börzsöny Mountains. After Visegrád it completes a final loop, thereafter settling on a north–south course. This whole stretch of the river – from Esztergom to Szentendre Island – is known as the Danube Bend, an area of enchantingly dramatic scenery.

ESZTERGOM

Esztergom is where King Stephen was born (c 975) and where he was crowned on Christmas Day, 1000. He founded Esztergom's archbishopric the following year; Hungarian Primates were based here until the Turkish conquest and returned only in the 19th century.

The Basilica

Hungary's largest church, begun in 1822 and completed in 1869, is more imposing than pleasing, but do not miss (to the left inside) the red marble funerary chapel (1507) of Archbishop Tamás Bakócz, a relic of the original cathedral here. The crypt contains some fine Renaissance sarcophagi and the *kincstár* (Treasury) has exquisite gold- and silversmiths' work.

Szent István tér 1. Tel: 06/33/311895. Basilica open: March to December, daily 9am–5pm; January and February, Tuesday to Sunday 7am–4pm. Treasury open: March to September, daily 9am–5pm; October to December 11am–4pm. Closed: January. Admission charges.

Vármúzeum (Medieval Royal Castle)

The old castle is just to the south of the basilica. It includes a 12th-century chapel with a fine rose window, the Hall of Virtues (so-called from the Italian frescos on its walls) and the room where Stephen was born.

Szent István tér 1. Tel: 06/33/311821. Open: Tuesday to Sunday 9am–5pm. Admission charge.

Keresztény Múzeum (Christian Museum)

This is in the Víziváros (Water Town). Its greatest treasure is the Lord's Coffin of Garamszentbenedek (c1480), which was paraded in Easter processions carrying the figure of Christ crucified. *Mindszenty tér 2. Tel: 06/33/ 313880. Open: March to September, Tuesday to Sunday 9am–5pm; October to December, Tuesday to Sunday 11am–4pm. Admission charge.*

Esztergom is 64km from Budapest on Road 11. Hourly buses from Árpád híd. Trains from Nyugati pályaudvar. A hydrofoil leaves at 9am on summer weekends from Vigadó tér.

VISEGRÁD

Királyi palota (Royal Palace)

Charles Robert of Anjou put Visegrád on the map by building a palace here in 1316. Enlarged and embellished by Sigismund of Luxembourg and Matthias Corvinus in the 15th century, it was rediscovered in the 1930s. The remains are on four levels. You will notice Matthias's coat of arms on the Herkules Fountain, the base of which may be seen here (the rest is in Solomon's Tower, see below). The Lion Fountain (a replica) is so-called because sleeping lions support the five columns of the baldachino. The lion's mouth of the fountain itself spouted wine when the king was in festive mood.

Fő utca 23. Tel: 06/26/398026. Open: April to October, Tuesday to Sunday 9am–4.30pm; November to March, 8am–3.30pm. Admission charge.

Salomon-torony (Solomon's Tower)

The tower was built two centuries after Salomon, son of Andrew I, was imprisoned in Visegrád, so the name is a

Esztergom – birthplace of King Stephen

romantic invention. It houses a museum with remnants from the royal palace. *Mátyás Király Múzeum (King Matthias Museum). Tel: 06/26/398026. Open: May to September, Tuesday to Sunday 9am–4.30pm. Admission charge.*

It is well worth climbing to the Fellegvár (Citadel, open daily 9am–5pm; tel: 26/ 398101) on the path from Nagy Lajos utca. The Hungarian crown jewels were once kept in this powerful fortress on a 350m-high peak. The views over the river and of the Börzsöny Mountains are superb.

Visegrád is 52km from Budapest and reached by buses from Árpád híd, or via Road 11 by car. Twice-daily boats run from Vigadó tér in summer.

The Basilica in Esztergom

KECSKEMÉT AND THE ALFÖLD (Hungarian Plain)

KECSKEMÉT

Kecskemét flourished as part of the Sultan's personal possessions during the Turkish occupation. In the 19th century it was fortunate when its vines were the only ones in Hungary to escape the phylloxera plague, and the town's wealth is reflected in its ambitious architecture and thriving cultural scene. The birthplace of the composer Zoltán Kodály and the father of Hungarian drama József Katona, it is also the production centre of the celebrated *barackpálinka* (apricot schnapps).

The main sights are clustered around the three central squares (Szabadság, Kossuth Lajos and Katona József terek). Where Rákóczi út enters Szabadság tér, on the left is Géza Márkus's Cifra-palota (Ornate Palace, 1902), a dazzling Jugendstil building. Opposite it is the Moorish-looking former synagogue (1862), converted in 1966 into a 'House of Science and Culture'. The Town Hall, designed by Ödön Lechner and Gyula Pártos should not be missed (open: Monday to Friday 10–11am, admission charge). Its carillon of 37 bells plays at 12.05pm, 6.05pm and 8.05pm.
Kecskemét is 85km south of Budapest and reachable by train (from Nyugati pályaudvar) and bus (from Népstadion terminal). By car take M5 and Road 5.

Lajosmizse is north of Kecskemét on Road 5. Shows 12.30pm daily in summer. Bugac is to the south – turn left at Kiskúnfélegyháza. IBUSZ (tel: 342–0583) and COOPTOURIST (tel: 166–5349) in Budapest organise tours.

THE ALFÖLD

Commonly referred to as the '*Puszta*' ('abandoned'), the once forested Great Plain was heavily depopulated under the Turks and during the 18th century. Regulation of the River Tisza in the 19th century deprived the land of its yearly alluvial deposits and turned it into the

alkaline pasture that covers most of the region today. *Puszta* traditions may be savoured at Lajosmizse and Bugac (both close to Kecskemét), where the *csikósok* (cowboys) give displays of horsemanship. At Bugac there is a Puszta Museum. You may also see the grey steppe cattle and the woolly *racka* sheep.

Helytörténeti Múzeum (Local History Museum)

Aspects of the local Cumanian culture and *puszta* fauna and flora are on display in the town of Kunszentmiklós. *Kossuth Lajos utca 3. Tel: 06/76/ 351353. Open: Tuesday, Friday and Sunday 9am–noon; Wednesday and Saturday 2–5pm. Road 51.*

BUDAPEST EXCURSIONS

PÉCS

The attractive city of Pécs was founded by the Celts, and subsequently (as *Sopianae*) became the capital of the Roman province of Pannonia Valeria. King Stephen established a bishopric here in 1009. Under the Turkish occupation Pécs was a centre of Islamic culture, boasting five *madrasahs* (seminaries) and 17 mosques. In the 18th century viticulture thrived and coal deposits were discovered, then in the 19th century the city boomed as a result of leather and other industries. Uranium mines were discovered close by in the 1950s.

Remains of the early Christian church in Pécs

The Cathedral at Pécs

The Cathedral

The huge neo-Romanesque cathedral above Szent István tér was given its present form by the Viennese architect, Friedrich Schmidt, between 1882 and 1891, but there are 11th-, 12th- and 14th-century remnants. Inside are 19th-century frescos by Bertalan Székely, Károly Lotz and others. In the Corpus Christi Chapel look for the Pastoforium of Bishop Szatmáry, a lovely Renaissance altar (1521) in red marble.

Roman remains

Pécs has some of the earliest Christian sanctuaries in Hungary. The Roman tombs at Apáca utca 9 and the remains of the *cella trichora* (clover-leaf chapel) on the opposite side of the street are not always accessible; but the mausoleum (AD350), just to the north on Szent István tér, is open. It contains frescos of the Fall and Daniel in the Lion's Den.

Turkish remains

Hungary's best preserved Turkish monuments are here. The most impressive is the Mosque of Gazi Kasim Pasha, built in 1579 using the stones of an earlier Christian church. To the west of the town centre is the Mosque of Jakovali Hassan Pasha with a finely carved *minbar* (pulpit). At Nyár utca 8 to the west is a *türbe* (sepulchral chapel, 1591) housing an exhibition concerning Turkish death rites. Near by is the only surviving Turkish fountain.

The Mosque of Gazi Kasim Pasha (right)

Csontváry Museum – Janus Pannonius utca 11–13. Tel: 06/72/310172. Open: Tuesday to Sunday 10am–6pm.
Mausoleum – Szent István tér. Tel: 72/311526. Open: April to October 10am–6pm; November to March 10am–4pm.
Mosque of Gazi Kasim Pasha – Széchenyi tér. Open: summer, Monday to Saturday 10am–4pm, Sunday 11.30am–4pm; winter, Monday to Saturday 11am–noon, Sunday 11.30am–2pm.
Mosque of Jakovali Hassan Pasha – Rákóczi út 2. Open: 1 May to 15 October, Tuesday to Sunday 10am–4pm.
Türbe of Idris Baba – Nyár utca 8. Tel: 06/72/325266. Open by request only.
Zsolnay Museum – Káptalan utca 2. Tel: 06/72/325266. Open: Tuesday to Sunday, 10am–6pm.
Admission charge to all sights.

Other sights

The Bishop's Palace, on Dóm tér is fronted by a modern statue of Franz Liszt. From the other side of the square you enter Káptalan utca through an archway. The street contains no less than five museums, of which the Zsolnay Museum (ceramics) is the most interesting. The others are devoted to individual artists except one featuring 20th-century Hungarian art. Walk along Kossuth Lajos utca to see the restored Jugendstil Hotel Palatinus and the neo-rococo theatre, home to Pest's Ballet Sopianae. In Jókai utca is a splendid Zsolnay well, whose lion's-head spout is copied from the so-called 'Treasure of Attila' discovered in Romania (now in Vienna). The works of Tivadar Csontváry Kosztka (1853–1919), in the Csontváry Museum, express a mystical vision of self and nation. Don't miss his great Baalbeck canvas and the poignant *Lonely Cedar*.

Pécs is 180km south of Budapest. Trains run direct from Budapest's Déli or Keleti pályaudvar. Buses leave from Erzsébet tér.

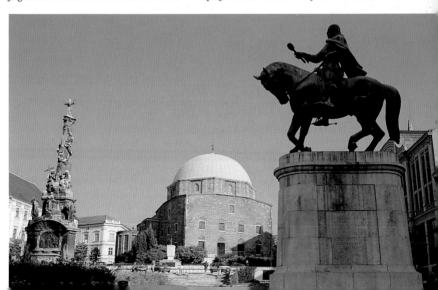

SZENTENDRE

Szentendre (St Andrew) has a Balkan charm rarely encountered in Hungary. It was founded as a town for Serbian refugees after the catastrophic defeat of Serbia by the Turks at Kosovo in 1389. A second wave of immigrants came in 1690, fleeing the wrath of the Turks after an abortive uprising. Both the earlier Hungarian kings and the Habsburgs favoured these refugees from the south. The settlers were able to exploit their trading privileges and the town's proximity to the Danube to become wealthy. Several Orthodox churches were built here in the 18th century, usually on the site of wooden predecessors, each representing a community drawn from a common provenance in the Slav homeland.

The Serb population has dwindled in the 20th century and now only about 100 are left out of Szentendre's 20,000 inhabitants. Some of the churches have been sold and are difficult to access.

Szentendre's other claim to fame is the artists' colony started here at the turn of the century and still going strong.

Service in an Orthodox church

CHURCHES

Belgrád székesegyház (Belgrade Cathedral)

The episcopal church is open only at times of mass (Sunday 10am, sometimes Saturday at 5 or 6pm). The iconostasis (1777), the bishop's throne and the pulpit are notable. Do not miss the nearby Szerb Egyházművészeti Gyűjtemény (Collection of Ecclesiastical Treasures) which contains fine icons and other works by Orthodox masters.
Pátriárka utca 5. Tel: 06/26/312399. Open: May to September, Wednesday to Sunday 10am–6pm; October to November and March to April 10am–4pm. December to February, Friday to Sunday 10am–4pm. Admission charge.

Blagoveštenska Church (Church of the Annunciation)

Commissioned by Greek merchants and built by Andreas Mayerhoffer (1754), this church has a fine iconostasis (1804) by a Serb artist from Buda.
Edge of Fő tér. Open: most days 9am–5pm. Admission charge.

Plébániatemplom (Parish Church of St John)

Steps lead up from Fő tér to Templom tér, on which stands the church of the Catholic Dalmatian community. You can only view it from the porch, but it is worth the climb for the marvellous panorama of the town from the square.

Požarevačka Church (Church of St Michael the Archangel)

The church was built in 1763 on the site of a wooden predecessor. Here and in the Blagoveštenska an atmospheric tape of Orthodox chant is played for the benefit of visitors.
Kossuth Lajos utca. Open: in summer,

Friday, Saturday and Sunday 11am–5pm.
Admission charge.

OTHER SIGHTS
Ferenczy Museum
Situated in the former Serbian school,
the museum is devoted to artistic works
by the Ferenczy family, of whom the
father, Károly (1862–1917), was the
leading figure in the Nagybánya artists'
colony (see pages 42–3).
Fő tér 6. Tel: 06//26/310244. Open: 16
March to 31 October 10am–5.30pm;
1 November to 15 March, Friday to
Sunday, 10am–4pm. Closed: Monday.
Admission charge.

Margit Kovács Museum
Billed as Hungary's leading ceramicist,
Margit Kovács (1902–77) made
sculpture and reliefs that drew
eclectically on the traditions of folk art
and fine art. The claims made for her
work have been recklessly inflated.
Vastagh György utca 1. Tel: 06/26/310244.
Open: 16 March to 31 October 9am–7pm;
1 November to 15 March 10am–4pm.
Closed: Monday. Admission charge.

View from the main square

Szabadtéri Néprajzi Múzeum
(Village Museum or Skanzen)
Known as a *skanzen* after a pioneering
Swedish ethnographical reconstruction
of village life and architecture, the
museum will eventually show typical
peasant dwellings, churches and
functional agricultural buildings from 10
regions of Hungary. At weekends there
are often demonstrations of crafts and
folklore programmes.
4km west of Szentendre on Szabadságforrás
út. Tel: 06/26/312304. Open: April to
October, Tuesday to Sunday 9am–5pm.
Hourly buses from HÉV station.

Szentendre is 23km northwest of Budapest.
There is a direct rail link (HÉV) from
Batthyány tér and hourly buses from Árpád
híd bus terminus. In summer boats leave
from Vigadó tér.

Margit Kovács Museum

The village of Zsámbék

Nyugati pályaudvar. Vac-Bottyán Múzeum – Múzeum utca 4, tel: 06/27/315064; open Tuesday to Sunday 10am–5pm. Admission charge.

VÁCRÁTÓT

This fascinating botanical garden comprises 12,000 species of plants and trees, artificial lakes, follies and a watermill.

25km north of Budapest. Infrequent trains from Nyugati pályaudvar. By car, take Road 2 to Szödliget and turn right. Tel: 06/27/360122; open April to October, 8am–6pm; November to March until 4pm; admission charge.

ZEBEGÉNY

Károly Kós's vernacular church is the main sight in this artists' haunt beside the Danube. The stylised frescos (*Emperor Constantine's Vision of the Cross, Saint Helena Discovering the True Cross*) are by the Gödöllő artist, Aladár Körösfői-Kriesch (see page 69).

50km north of Budapest. Roads 2 and 12 via Vác; very slow boats from Vigadó tér in summer.

ZSÁMBÉK

The ruined Romanesque and Late Gothic church here was built for the Premonstratensians in the 13th century and later taken over by the Paulites. Another attraction is the Lamp Museum, housed in a typical Swabian cottage (the village was Swabian until the expulsion of many Germans following World War II).

33km west of Budapest. Buses from Széna tér (next to Moszkva tér). Lamp Museum – Magyar utca 18, tel: 06/23/342212; open daily 8am–6pm; admission charge.

VÁC

Mentioned by Ptolemy in his Geographia, the ancient town of Vác was made an episcopal See by King Stephen. The town was rich – the Vác silver mark was the main local currency of the 14th century – and the bishops were powerful. One of them, Kristóf Migazzi, had the Triumphal Arch near Március 15 tér erected for Maria Theresa's visit in 1764. Its architect, Isidore Canevale, built the imposing neo-classical cathedral on Konstantin tér in 1777. It contains a fine fresco (*The Trinity* by Franz Anton Maulbertsch) in its cupola.

Worth seeing also are the Dominican Church (Március 15 tér) and the Vak-Bottyán Museum.

34km north of Budapest. Trains from

GETTING AWAY
FROM IT ALL

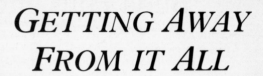

'Budapest and the Danube
present one of the most beautiful
river-town landscapes
anywhere: perhaps the most
beautiful in Europe, on a par
with London and the Thames
or Paris and the Seine.'
JULES ROMAINS,
1926

Buda Hills and Caves

BUDA CAVES

A number of exciting caves have been
discovered in the Buda Hills, and four of
them can be visited without difficulty.
Ancient and long inactive vents for hot
springs, the caves have been formed
along tectonic fractures.

Castle Hill Caves

The interior of Castle Hill is
honeycombed with caves which were
structurally improved by the inhabitants
over the years. Remnants of Palaeolithic
culture have been found here. The 10km
of passages and chambers were used in

World War II as an air-raid shelter and
field hospital. A gruesome waxworks
exhibition (Budavári Panoptikum)
illustrating the bloodiest scenes of
Hungarian history now occupies a part of
them.
*Úri utca 9. Tel: 175–6858. Open:
Wednesday to Monday 10am–6pm.
Admission charge. Buses 16, 116 or várbusz
to Dísz tér.*

Gellért-hegy Cave (Rock Chapel)

The earliest human habitation of the
region was probably in the Gellért caves.
A chapel consecrated here in 1926 was
walled up by the Communists but
reopened in 1990.
*Szent Gellért rakpart 1. Tel: 385–1529.
Trams 19, 47, 49. Bus 86 to Szent Gellért
tér.*

Pálvölgyi Barlang

This 7km-long cave came to light in
1902 when the son of the local quarry
manager squeezed himself through a gap
in the rocks. The highlight of the tour is
the 'zoo', so-called because the drip
formations recall elephants and
crocodiles.
*Szépvölgyi út 162. Tel: 325–9505. Open:
April to October, Tuesday to Saturday
10am–6pm. Admission charge. Bus 65 (five
stops) from Kolosy tér, Óbuda.*

Szemlőhegyi Barlang

This is renowned for its 'peastone'
formations like bunches of grapes, with
little stalactites suspended from them.
Part of the cave is used for treating
people with respiratory diseases. There is

Rock Chapel in Gellért Hill

At the ticket offices for the Pálvölgyi and Szemlőhegyi caves you can apply to join special tours of several other caves not normally open to the public. Appropriate dress will be provided. It is a prerequisite that you be fit and in sound health.

a small exhibition about local speleology in the reception building.
Pusztaszeri út 35. Tel: 325–6001. Open: Wednesday to Monday 9am–4pm. Admission charge. Bus 29 (four stops) from Kolosy tér, Óbuda.

The Children's Railway

BUDAI-HEGYSÉG
(The Buda Hills)
The easiest way of seeing the Buda Hills is to make a tour with the cogwheel railway and the Children's (formerly 'Pioneer') Railway (see page 154).

The cogwheel railway (Fogaskerekű Vasút) ascends from Városmajor along wooded slopes past the Svábhegy (a Swabian village founded under Maria Theresa), and the Pető Institute for helping brain-damaged children, to Regé út on Széchenyi-hegy. Near by is the end-station for the Children's Railway (Gyermekvasút), so-called because it is staffed by children under the supervision of adults. You can take it to the terminus at Hűvösvölgy, or get off at Normafa (first stop) or János-hegy (fourth stop) for rambles with convenient return connections. From Normafa a 2km walk (bear left) brings you to the Budakeszi Game Park (deer, moufflon, many bird species), with return buses to Moszkva tér. From János-hegy (529m, look-out tower) a chairlift descends to Zugligeti út (bus 158 to Moszkva tér).

For the cogwheel railway take trams 18, 56, bus 56 from Moszkva tér along Szilágyi Erzsébet fasor to the stop opposite the Hotel Budapest. The Children's Railway runs half-hourly 9am–6.30pm in summer, 9am–5pm in winter. Budakeszi Game Park open: daily 9am–5pm (direct connection with bus 22 from Moszkva tér to Korányi Sanatorium). The János-hegy chairlift operates 9am–5pm or 9.30am–4pm according to season.

Waxworks in the Castle Hill caves

Danube Islands

Of the islands on the Budapest stretch of the Danube, the small Óbuda Island is largely of historical interest: a shipyard was founded here in 1836 on the initiative of Count Széchenyi, and still operates, although under threat due to the collapse of Russian demand for river craft. At the north end are the ruins of the Roman governor's palace. The Margaret Island is the city's loveliest park (see page 48 for details and pages 108–9 for a walk around it). Csepel Island begins in Budapest and extends to the Great Hungarian Plain.

CSEPEL-SZIGET
(Csepel Island)

This elongated sliver of land begins as Budapest's industrialised 21st District and ends 54km to the south. The origins of the district's heavy industry go back to 1882 when Manfred Weiss founded a factory producing ration tins for troops of the Austro-Hungarian army. He moved to Csepel in 1890 and expanded into armaments. The Communists nationalised the business after the war and the workers of 'Red Csepel' were supposed to be a bulwark of proletarian solidarity (they even had the dubious pleasure of being represented by the Stalinist dictator Rákosi). Nevertheless, they were the last to hold out against Russian tanks in the 1956 revolution.

Façade at Ráckeve

Csepel's industry is now largely obsolete and it is planned to use some of its vacant lots for exhibitions and the like. In 1993 the islanders voted narrowly in a plebiscite to break away from Budapest, but the result has no constitutional validity.

RÁCKEVE

The place most worth visiting on Csepel Island lies to the south, where the subtopian industrial suburbs have given way to cottages and gardens. Rác means Serb in Hungarian, and the small town was originally populated by Serbs from Keve, who fled here in the 15th century. Of Ráckeve's 1,800 inhabitants, only a handful are now Serb.

Szerb Templom (Serbian Church)

Ráckeve's church survives and is well worth a visit. The main Gothic structure dates to 1487, but the two side-chapels were added later, together with a baroque spire. Inside are colourful frescos (1771) in Byzantine style by Tódor Gruntovic (who was apparently an Albanian from Kosovo). The sequence begins to the right of the entrance with the Nativity and continues round the church walls, ending with the Resurrection. The baroque iconostasis

Prince Eugene of Savoy's elegant mansion at Ráckeve

(1768) is also striking.
Viola utca 1. Tel: 06/24/385985. Open:
Tuesday to Saturday 10am–noon, 2–5pm;
Sunday 2–5pm.

Savoyai Kastély (Mansion of Prince Eugene of Savoy)

The land on which this delightfully elegant mansion was built originally belonged to the Habsburgs and was sold by them to Prince Eugene after the Turkish wars. He employed Johann Lukas von Hildebrandt (later to build the magnificent Belvedere Palace in Vienna for him) to construct a baroque Schloss between 1702 and 1722. The neo-classical dome was added in the 19th century. The splendid interiors have unfortunately been destroyed and the mansion is now a smart hotel.
Kossuth-Lajos utca 95. Hotel – tel: 06/24/385253.

Ráckeve is 46km south of Budapest. The
HÉV suburban train leaves from Közvágóhíd
terminus in Pest and takes 75 minutes.

PRINCE EUGENE OF SAVOY
The greatest general in the history of Central Europe, Prince Eugene was responsible for clearing Hungary of the Turks after participating in the reconquest of Buda (1686). The Battle of Zenta (1697) was decisive in removing the Ottoman menace once and for all. Eugene was no less successful when allied with the Duke of Marlborough against the French in the War of the Spanish Succession (1701–14). His statue (originally commissioned by the people of Zenta) stands before the National Gallery on Castle Hill.

WEKERLE-TELEP (Wekerle Settlement)

In the 19th District (Kispest) a remarkable experiment in 20th-century social housing reflects the ambitious plans for city expansion developed under Budapest's most successful mayor, István Bárczy. Inspired by the principles of the English garden suburb, the Wekerle Housing Estate was built over 20 years from 1909 as a completely self-contained village for employees of the municipality. It consists of 650 single-storey villas and 270 bungalows and bears the name of Sándor Wekerle, the far-sighted and liberal prime minister between 1892 and 1895, and again between 1906 and 1910. Wekerle

KÁROLY KÓS (1883–1977)

Born in Temesvár (now Romanian Timisoara) in Transylvania, Kós won major commissions in Budapest when still in his twenties. As an architect he was influenced by Finnish architecture and the English Arts and Crafts movement. He was also a gifted writer, illustrating and printing his own works. In Budapest, in addition to the Wekerle Settlement, he designed the buildings for the zoo in 'national romantic style'; dwelling houses that recall the work of Arts and Crafts architect, Charles Voysey, in England; and schools and churches in vernacular style.

Wekerle Settlement

reformed the Hungarian currency and successfully fought to limit clerical influence in matters that should be the prerogative of the state.

The principal architect for the estate was the polymath Károly Kós (see above), who invested the wooden gabled and balconied houses with a Transylvanian charm (albeit pseudo). Four ornamental gates stand at the entrances to the central Kós Károly tér. The west gate is particularly interesting, consisting of a huge planked gable rising over rusticated plinths. Another gate mixes picturesque vernacular decoration with Renaissance features.

The houses have their own vegetable gardens – a rarity within the city – and the different quarters are divided by leafy avenues and squares.

Metro (blue line) to Határ út; then bus 194 to Kós Károly tér.

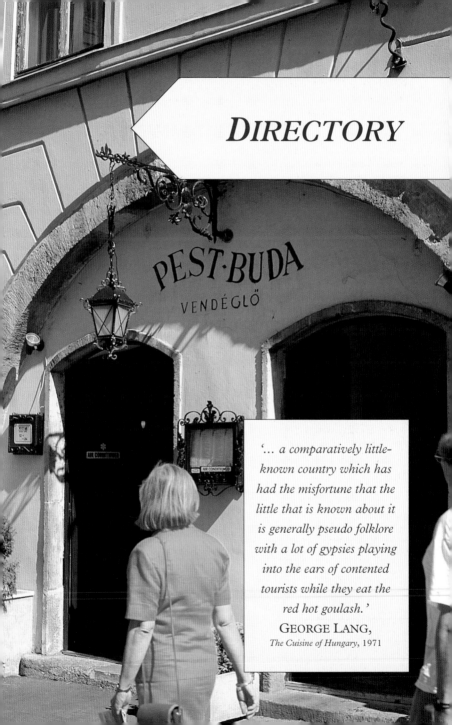

DIRECTORY

'... a comparatively little-known country which has had the misfortune that the little that is known about it is generally pseudo folklore with a lot of gypsies playing into the ears of contented tourists while they eat the red hot goulash.'

GEORGE LANG,
The Cuisine of Hungary, 1971

Shopping

*T*he main shopping area is the celebrated Váci utca (see page 86) in the heart of Pest. Here you will find long-established Hungarian shops selling such items as folk art or books alongside newcomers like Adidas and branches of Austrian chain stores. Souvenir-hunters will find plenty to interest them on Castle Hill, while the Fortuna Passage opposite the Hilton has a good book-shop, together with boutiques selling embroidery and antiques. Other items to look out for are Herend porcelain and Zsolnay faience. Food delicacies include salami, goose liver and Tokaji wine.

Tourist-orientated shops accept the usual credit cards, but the majority of places take only cash.

ANTIQUES
The state-owned chain **Bizományi Áruház Vállalat (BÁV)** is the best bet for reasonably priced antiques and furniture. There are branches at:
Szent István körút 3. Tel: 131–4534.
Ferenciek tere 3. Tel: 118–3381.
Hess András tér 3 (Castle Hill).
Tel: 175–0392.

Other antique shops:
Antikvitás
Vitkovics Mihály utca 3–5.
Tel: 117–6289.
Qualitás Antiquités
Kígyó utca 5. Tel: 118–3246.

Relikvia
Fortuna utca 14 (Castle Hill).
Tel: 175–6971.

ART GALLERIES
Csók István Galéria
Váci utca 25. Tel: 118–2592.
Deák Gallery
Attila út 35. Tel: 375–6015.
Gallerie Blitz
Falk Miksa utca 3. Tel: 132–0401.

CHILDREN'S WEAR
Benjamin
Kossuth Lajos utca 3. Tel: 117–4061.
Mari gyermekruhaüzlet
Váci utca 44. Tel: 137–4126.

DELICATESSENS
La Boutique des Vins
The owner is chef of the famous Gundel Restaurant.
József Attila utca 12. Tel: 117–5919.
Julius Meinl
All branches of this classic grocers' chain are good, this one outstanding.
Rákóczi út 50. Tel: 322–0069.
Mézeskalács bolt
Gingerbread figures and honey-cake.
Országház utca 8 (Castle Hill).
Tel: 156–0553.

Antiques can be very good value

DEPARTMENT STORES
Fontana
Váci utca 16. Tel: 266–6400.
Luxus
Vörösmarty tér 3. Tel: 118–3550.

FASHION
Betty Barclays
Petőfi Sándor utca 2. Tel: 118–3238.
Böne Kft – Levi's Store
Baross tér 18. Tel: 322–5259.
Clara Szalon
Váci utca 12. Tel: 118–4090.

FOLK ART
Attractive items include Kalocsa
embroidery, Halas lace, Haban faience,
wax figures and painted Easter eggs.

Lux Folklor
Váci utca 6. Tel: 318–6980.
Népművészeti bolt
Rákóczi út 32. Tel: 342–0753.
**Népművészeti és Háziipari
Szövetkezet**
Régiposta utca 12. Tel: 266–5334.

FOREIGN LANGUAGE BOOKSHOPS
Bestsellers
English and American books and
newspapers
V Október 6 utca 11. Tel: 312–1295.
Corvina
Kossuth Lajos utca 4. Tel: 118–3603.
Litea Bookshop and Tea-Garden
*Hess András tér 4 (Fortuna Passage).
Tel: 375–6987.*
**Párizsi Udvar Idegennyelvű
Könyvesbolt**
*Petőfi Sándor utca 2 (Paris Arcade).
Tel: 318–3136.*

There are several others in and around
Váci utca.

GLASS AND PORCELAIN
Goda Kustály
Kígyó utca 5. Tel: 118–3324.
Special Hungarian Gifts
Váci utca 23. Tel: 318–3240.
Zsolnay Márkabolt
Kígyó utca 4. Tel: 118–3712.

JEWELLERY
Art Gold
Madách Imne út 10. Tel: 342–6239.
Orimex Ékszerbolt
Kálvin tér 1. Tel: 118–3692.
Richter Károly
*Országház utca 12 (Castle Hill).
Tel: 356–1746.*

MUSIC
Concerto
Classical music specialist.
Dob utca 33. Tel 121–6432.
Hungaroton
Classical and pop music from Hungary.
Vörösmarty tér 1. Tel: 117–6222.
Rózsavölgyi Zeneműbolt
Szervita tér 5. Tel: 118–3500.

PRINTS AND MAPS
Cartographia
Largest selection of current local and
foreign maps.
*Bajcsy-Zsilinszky út 37.
Tel: 312–6001.*
Központi Antikvárium
Old prints; also second-hand books.
Múzeum körút 13–15. Tel: 117–3781.

SHOES
Vass Handmade Shoes Ltd
Haris köz 2. Tel: 118–2375.

SOUVENIRS
Idea
*Úri utca 26 (Castle Hill).
Tel: 355–9202.*

Markets

FLEA MARKETS

The legendary flea markets (*bolhapiac*) of Budapest, though not for the faint-hearted, are a paradise for junk fanatics. Since the collapse of Communism the amount of Marxist-Leninist tat to be found in them has notably increased; there are even Russian army uniforms and caps, sold off by impoverished Soviet troops before their departure.

Ecseri Piac (Ecseri Flea Market)

This was officially renamed Használtcikk ('Used Items') market after one of its several moves from its original location on Ecseri út, but everyone uses the old name. The outer stalls (*kirakodó*) are loaded with bric-à-brac – most of it uninspiring, the good stuff having been sold to dealers in the early hours. These dealers (many of them Slavs or gypsies) occupy booths in the centre, and it is here that you might find bargains. Much of their stock comes from peasants, persuaded to part with their family heirlooms when the dealers canvassed a village.

The most interesting goods at Ecseri are decorative silver and Russian icons. Unfortunately the silver is usually being sold illegally (under Hungarian law a permit is required to deal in it), while the icons may well have been looted from Ukrainian churches. Not long ago the police confiscated some icons that had been stolen from somewhere near Chernobyl – on the grounds that they were contaminated with radiation, not because they were stolen! Other items of interest said to crop up include 'bentwood' chairs made by the Viennese Thonet company, old radios and copper lamps.

It is best to go to Ecseri with a

Vegetables on display

Hungarian who knows the ropes and you should beware of pickpockets.

Nagykőrösi út 156 in the 19th District. Open: Monday to Friday 8am–4pm, Saturday 8am–3pm. Bus 54 from Boráros tér.

Józsefvárosi piac (Market in the Józsefváros)

In the summer of 1993 the famous Kelenföldi flea market closed down, but to everyone's relief opened shortly afterwards in a new location. The self-styled 'Worldwide Business Centre' is really a Third World souk. Traders come from as far afield as China and Vietnam, but chiefly from the former Soviet Union, Bulgaria and Romania. They trade cheap goods for things not available back home. American kitsch is big here, as are liquor of uncertain provenance, used car parts, cigarette lighters – anything, in short, that might have fallen off the back of a lorry or turned up in the attic.

Kőbányai út 9 (10th District). Tram 28 from Blaha Lujza tér or bus 9 from Deák Ferenc tér.

FOOD AND GENERAL MARKETS
Batthyány téri csarnok (The Market Hall on Batthyány tér)

Like the Central Market (see below) this one dates from the 1890s. It is basically a two-storey supermarket with private traders operating in the arcade at the front.

Batthyány tér 5–7. Tel: 202–5044. Open: Monday to Friday 6am–8pm, Saturday 7am–5pm, Sunday 7am–1pm. Metro to Batthyány tér.

Központi Vásárcsarnok (Central Market)

A visit to this fabulous 19th-century

Local flea market

covered market is strongly recommended. It was one of five opened in the 1890s (see page 113) and is a protected monument. There are over 100 stalls on two floors selling meat, vegetables, fruit and even flower seeds and pottery; note that most stalls close around noon.

Vámház körút 1–3 (temporarily moved to Fővám tér 12 during renovation). Tel: 217–6865. Open: Monday to Thursday 6am–4pm, Friday 6am–7pm, Saturday 6am–3pm. Trams 47, 49 to Fővám tér.

Western supermarkets have moved in on Budapest – including Spar and Tesco. Spar now have five branches and Tesco two: Pillangó utca 15 (tel: 467–6800) and Szentmihály út 131 (tel: 417–1988).

Entertainment

BALLET

Ballet is not a major feature of the
Budapest scene, but performances by
prima ballerinas Katalin Volf and Ildikó
Pongor are worth looking out for. The
corps de ballet is resident at the State
Opera (see below). Foreign companies
make guest appearances at Budapest arts
festivals (see page 149).

CINEMA

The cinematic tradition is strong in
Hungary and there are currently over 60
cinemas in Budapest. Works of the giants
of the Hungarian film scene – directors
such as Miklós Jancsó, Pál Sándor or
István Szabó – will be well-known to
western film buffs. Although the big co-
productions such as *Colonel Redl* or
Mephisto have been widely exposed
abroad, the occasional Budapest summer
seasons of home-grown movies afford a
chance to see more obscure works with
English subtitles. *Pesti Műsor* is the best

source for information on such events –
look under the heading *A budapesti
mozik műsora* (preferably with a
Hungarian friend on hand to translate).

Films in English, German, French
and Italian

With the lifting of censorship in 1989 a
tidal wave of American products – sex
'n' violence to the fore – engulfed the
Budapest movie screens. Now things
have settled down, you can see most
recent mainstream films with the
original soundtrack. The best sources of
information are the detailed movie
programmes in *Budapest Week* and *The
Budapest Sun*. Classics are shown at the
Filmmúzeum located in the Broadway
Cinema (Karóly körút 3, tel:
322–0230). There are usually some
seven or eight films in the repertory at
any one time.

Film posters

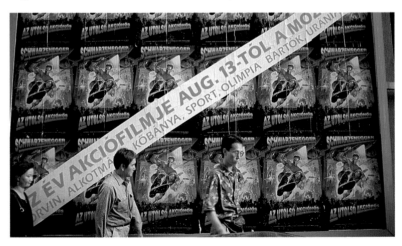

OPERA

Opera is popular in Hungary and has a distinguished tradition reaching back to the opening of Miklós Ybl's beautiful opera house in 1882 (see pages 66–7). New productions are put on during the spring music festival and the autumn/winter season.

If you want specifically to see Hungarian opera, look out for Béla Bartók's *Kékszakállú herceg vára* (*Bluebeard's Castle*), Ferenc Erkel's *Bánk Bán*, Károly Goldmark's *Sába királynője* (*The Queen of Sheba*) and Zoltán Kódaly's *Háry János*.

The State Opera went through a bad patch in the last phase of Communism due to incompetent management; the main problem today is lack of money. However, leading Hungarian expatriate singers (Sylvia Sass or Éva Marton, for instance) sometimes visit and are well worth the modest price of a ticket.

Opera venues

Magyar Állami Operaház (State Opera House)
Andrássy út 22. Tel: 153–0170. Box office at Andrássy út 18. Tel: 112–0000.
Erkel Színház (Erkel Theatre)
Köztársaság tér 30. Tel: 333–0540.

OPERETTA AND MUSICALS

The heyday of operetta followed the formation of the Austro-Hungarian Empire in 1867 and lasted until the end of World War I (see pages 70–1). It has been largely superseded by the musical, of which two popular Hungarian examples are the rock-operas *István, a király* (*Stephen the King*) and *Attila* (first produced in 1993).

Operetta venues

Fővárosi Operett Színház

Concert performance in the Vigadó

(Operetta Theatre)
Nagymezo utca 17. Tel: 269–3870.
Pesti Vigadó (The Pest Redoute)
From May to October, on Tuesday, Thursday and Saturday, the theatre offers a programme of hits from Lehár, Strauss, Kálmán and Ábrahám.
Vigadó tér 2. Tel: 118–9167.

Rock musical venues

Madách Színház (Madach Theatre)
Erzsébet körút 29–33. Tel: 322–0677.
Nemzeti Színház (National Theatre)
Hevesi Sándor tér 4. Tel: 322–0014.

THEATRE

The obvious problem about visiting the theatre in Budapest is the language barrier. The **Katona József Theatre** (Petőfi Sándor utca 6, tel: 118–6599) provides English language summaries of the plays on request. The **Merlin Theatre** (Gerlóczy utca 4, tel: 117–9338) is currently the only venue for English language productions, but they are few and far between.

Music

CLASSICAL MUSIC

The classical tradition in Hungary is very strong, not least because the Music Academy (see pages 68–9 and below) has been the breeding ground for generations of world-class talents. Names such as Széll, Solti, Doráti and Ormándy will be familiar to all music lovers. The new generation includes outstanding soloists such as Dezső Ránki and Zoltán Kocsis (piano), Vilmos Szabadi (violin) and Miklós Perényi (cello). The list of distinguished composers from such a small country is equally remarkable – Franz Liszt, Ferenc Erkel, Béla Bartók, Zoltán Kodály and Ernő Dohnányi. Two Hungarians who have had considerable impact on the modern music scene are György Ligeti and György Kurtág.

Main classical music venues
Budapest Kongresszusi Központ (Budapest Convention Centre)
A large modern concert hall away from the centre.
Jagelló út 1–3. Tel: 209–4850.
Erdődy-palota (Erdody Palace)
Concerts in the Museum of the History of Music (see page 64).
Táncsics Mihály utca 7. Tel: 214–677/250.
Hilton Szálló (Dominican Courtyard of the Hilton Hotel)
Pleasant chamber music concerts in summer.
Hess András tér 1–3. Tel: 118–9167.
Pesti Vigadó (The Pest Redoute)
Famous for its poor acoustics! (See pages 68 and 147.)
Vigadó tér 2. Tel: 118–9167.
A Városháza Díszterme (Ceremonial Chamber, City Hall)
The chamber concerts are a good excuse to view the interior of this fine building.
Városház utca 11. Tel: 318–6066.
Zeneakadémia (Music Academy)
Highly recommended for acoustics and exotic architecture (see pages 68–9).
Liszt Ferenc tér 8. Tel: 342–0179.

Organ and choral performances are also held in the Matthias Church and St Stephen's Basilica.

FOLK MUSIC
Budai Vigadó (The Buda Redoute)
Home of the State Folk Ensemble.
Corvin tér 4. Tel: 201–5928.
Fővárosi Művelődési Ház (City Cultural House)
Easily the best group for Hungarian folk

Concert poster

The Music Academy

music (Muzsikás with Márta Sebestyén)
plays here on Tuesdays.
Fehérvári út 47. Tel: 203–3868.

FESTIVALS

The first important music month of the
year is March, with the Budapest Spring
Festival during its second half. The
festival claims to offer '10 days of 1,000
events in 100 venues', and many big-
name musicians make guest appearances.

Summer sees performances on the
open-air stages of the city (notably opera
at the Margaret Island Theatre, tel:

340–5540) and at venues within striking
distance of the capital (for example at the
country house at Martonvásár). Baroque
operas are now being performed each
summer in the courtyard of the Zichy
Palace in Óbuda. There is an autumn
Festival of Church Music, which
provides a good chance to hear
interesting works by Hungarian
composers from earliest times to the
present. In November a choral festival
with the title *Vox Pacis* takes place. The
number of events and mini-festivals is
continually increasing with sponsorship.

GYPSIES AND THEIR MUSIC

Gypsies first came to Hungary in the 15th century and are now the largest minority in the country (5 per cent of the population); they are also the most underprivileged. In the public mind they are associated less with music than with poverty, crime and unemployment. To combat this a 'Roma Parliament' was recently formed, and its leaders are trying to raise national consciousness and improve the gypsies' tainted image.

the *Gypsy Bandleader* (1912). In the late 19th century the *Neue Freie Presse* in Vienna pointed out how members of gypsy musician families had benefited from the Hungarian gypsy cult: 'They no longer tell fortunes or ply the tinker's trade, but instead put on a dinner jacket and fiddle for the *beau monde* from eleven at night till five in the morning'.

Contrary to popular belief, what the musicians play is not the true music of

Traditional gypsy music and dance

Music has traditionally offered gypsies a way out of the cultural ghetto. Gypsy players accompanied conscription drives across the land in the 18th century; gypsy bands played for the nobility and the gentry in the 19th century, when they began to become figures of romance. Around the turn of the century they were romanticised in operettas like *Gypsy Life* (1904), *Gypsy Love* (1910) and

the gypsies. According to the composer Béla Bartók, 'They are simply performers of Hungarian popular song'; and he added: 'There is of course gypsy music – songs with texts in gypsy language. These are never played or sung by gypsies in public.'

Today the smarter restaurants in Budapest all have their own gypsy ensemble playing evergreens from Viennese operetta and the frenzied Hungarian *csárdás*. These are the aristocrats of the gypsy world, famous for their ready wit and happy-go-lucky temperament, unextinguished by centuries of persecution.

Nightlife

*B*udapest's nightlife has thrown aside the prudery and inhibitions of the Communist era, and now offers a range of floor shows, clubs and discos. These last tend to come and go – the ones mentioned below look to have staying power, but there is no guarantee. Most places exact an entry fee or cover charge and drinks can be quite expensive by local standards. In general the average traveller might find the jazz locales more congenial than the rock venues; floor shows are better in the hotels than elsewhere.

CASINOS

Budapest Casino
Situated in the tower of the Hilton Hotel. Roulette, Black Jack, video games. Hard currency only (preferably Deutschmarks).
Hess András tér 1–3. Tel: 156–4982. Open: 5pm–2am.

Casino Lido
Roulette, Black Jack, Red Dog. Gambling with hard currency, food and drink payable in forints.
Szabadsajtó út 5. Tel: 118–2404. Open: midnight–5am.

Várhert Casino
Sophisticated casino in the former Ybl 'kiosk' (pumphouse for the Royal Castle).
Ybl Miklós tér 9. Tel: 202–4244. Open: 5pm–2am.

DISCOS

Buddy Holly Club
A haven of (and for) golden oldies.
Bogdánffy út 10. Tel: 291–8966. Open: Fridays 9pm–4pm.

High Life Disco
Two discos in one place, techno rave downstairs, techno-free upstairs.
Kalap utca 4. Tel: 250–2979. Open: Friday and Saturday 9.30pm–7am.

Hully Gully
Laser shows and sexy go-go girls. Fashionable.
Apor Vilmos tér 9. Tel: 375–9742. Open: 9pm–5am (Wednesday to Friday free to women).

Mask Music Club
Concerts nightly at 10pm. Hip-hop, jazz and good pizzas.
Kertész utca 33. Tel: 267–8616. Open: until 1am weekdays, 4am Friday and Saturday.

Petőfi Csarnok
Lively and popular Saturday night disco with plenty of special effects.
Zichy Mihály utca 14. Tel: 251–7266.

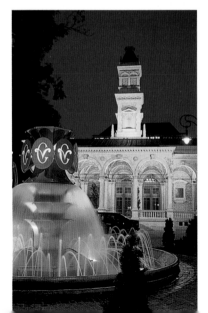

The 'Ybl Kiosk', now a casino

A typical floorshow, Pest-style

FLOOR SHOWS
Caligula
The name's promise of decadent entertainment draws the cognoscenti.
Szilágyi Erzsébet fasor 37–39. Tel: 212–3177. Open: 10pm–5am.
Maxim Varieté
In Hotel Emke (very expensive).
Akácfa utca 3. Tel: 122–7858. Open: Monday to Saturday 8pm–2am.

JAZZ
Attempts are being made to stimulate the jazz scene, which languished under Communism. An excellent initiative of the municipality was the founding of the Merlin Theatre and Jazz Café in 1990. The most enduringly popular local ensemble is the Benkó Dixieland Band.

Crazy Café
Basement with live jazz and blues.
Jókai utca 30. Tel: 269–5484. Open: evenings till 1am.
Hades Jazz Club
Speleological experience with tree (of life?) above the bar.
Vörösmarty utca 31. Tel: 352–1503. Open: Monday to Friday noon–2am; Saturday and Sunday 5pm–2am.
The Long Jazz Club
Authentic modern and swing.

Dohány utca 22–24. Tel: 322–0006. Programmes start at 9.30pm.
Merlin Jazz Club
Restaurant in Merlin Theatre. Local and foreign stars appear.
Gerlóczy utca 4. Tel: 317–9338. Performances 10pm and midnight, Friday to Sunday.

ROCK
Rolling Rock Café
Live music until the early hours.
Bécsi út 53–55. Tel: 368–2298. Open: until 5am.
Jamaica Jamming
Mainstream reggae.
Hungária körút 134. No telephone. Open: Sunday to Thursday 11pm–1am; Friday and Saturday 11pm–3am.
Rocktogon
Full of youthful trendies.
Mozsár utca 9. Tel: 353–0443. Open: Tuesday to Saturday 7pm–4am.

> For nightlife happenings, see the listings in the style section of the *Budapest Sun*, and the local weekly programme of events, *Pesti Műsor* (in Hungarian, published Thursdays). The Tourist Board issues a monthly *Programme* in English.

Children

*T*he suggestions below are for activities largely unaffected by the language barrier. Parents could also consider a visit to a stalactite cave or the Buda Hills (see pages 136–7) or, in summer, a boat trip on the Danube (apply to MAHART, Vigadó tér).

BÁBSZÍNHÁZ (Puppet Show)

There are two theatres: **Budapest Bábszínház**, Andrássy út 69 (tel: 321–5200; metro to Vörösmarty utca) and **Bábszínház**, Jókai tér 10 (tel: 112–0622; metro to Oktogon). Mainly international and Hungarian fairy tales.

BUDAVÁRI LABIRINTUS PANOPTIKUM (Waxworks in the Buda Labyrinth)

Gory version of Hungarian history. *Úri utca 9. Tel: 175–6858. Open: daily 9.30am–7.30pm. Admission charge. Várbusz to Szentháromság tér.*

GELLÉRT GYÓGYFÜRDŐ (Gellért Baths)

There are many other baths (see pages 32–3) but Gellért offers the bubble bath inside and the wave bath outside.

Kelenhegyi út 4–6. Tel: 166–6166. Open: daily.

GYERMEKVASÚT (Children's Railway)

Formerly the 'Pioneer Railway' of the Communist youth movement, running 12km between Széchenyi-hegy and Hűvösvölgy in the Buda Hills, it has been temporarily saved but its future is uncertain. The driver is adult but the staff are children (compulsory retirement age, 14).

Széchenyi-hegy is reached by the Fogaskerekű Vasút (cogwheel railway), whose terminus is opposite Hotel Budapest, Szilágyi Erzsébet fasor 47.

MARGITSZIGET (Margaret Island)

The various sights are described on pages 108–9; for children, bicycles and tricycles can be hired at the southern end, next to the Centennial Monument. At the northern end is the Japanese Garden with its waterfall and a 'singing well' that plays a tune each hour.

MUSEUMS

Bélyegmúzeum (Stamp Museum)

Eleven million stamps!
Hársfa utca 47. Tel: 341–5526. Open: Tuesday to Sunday 10am–6pm. Admission charge. Trolley bus 74.

Postsai és Távközlési Múzeum (Postal Museum)

Models, coaches and a message despatch tube to play with.

Luna Park in Városliget has plenty to occupy children

The Big Wheel

Andrássy út 3. Tel: 269–6838. Open: Tuesday to Sunday 10am–6pm. Admission charge. Metro to Deák Ferenc tér.

Telefónia Múzeum (Telephone Museum)

A rare museum that lets children play with the exhibits.

Úri utca 49. Tel: 201–8188. Open: Tuesday to Sunday 10am–5.30pm. Admission charge. Várbusz to Szentháromság tér.

The National Museum, Transport Museum and Museum of Military History have exhibits that might interest children and are dealt with in the museum section (see pages 60–5).

PLANETÁRIUM

Planets are projected on to a dome and there are laser shows with music, plus special shows for children.

Népliget. Tel: 265–0725. Times of shows vary. Admission charge. Metro to Népliget.

PLAY AREAS

Play areas are scarce on the Buda side, but one worth considering is Nagy Imre tér off Fő utca. On the Pest side the secluded Károlyi kert behind the Károlyi Palace on the street of the same name is

pleasant. Erzsébet tér is well equipped with climbing bars, sand-pits, etc.

VÁROSLIGET (City Woodland Park)

Many attractions for children include rowing on the pond (skating in winter) and a Lilliput train in summer. The zoo, circus and amusement park are rather shabby, but details follow.

Állatkert (Zoo)

Three thousand animals and a special children's corner.

Állatkerti körút 6–12. Tel: 343–6075. Open: 9am–6pm (4pm in winter).

Fővárosi Nagycirkusz (Circus)

Állatkerti körút 7. Tel: 343–6075. Shows: Wednesday to Friday 3pm and 7pm, Saturday and Sunday 10am and 3pm. Closed: Monday, Tuesday and 1 September to mid-October.

Vidám Park (Amusement Park)

Állatkerti körút 14-16. Tel: 343–0996. Open: 10am–8pm. Separate section for children.

Trolley bus 72 from the metro stop at Arany János utca or metro to Széchenyi fürdő brings you close to all three of the above locations.

The zoo in Városliget

Sport

Magyars are great football fans and Hungary has produced some charismatic players like Puskás. Otherwise they excel in sports such as swimming and water polo, no doubt helped by the top-class training facilities available.

SPECTATOR SPORTS
CYCLE RACING
There is a championship track with a capacity of 14,000 for cycle racing enthusiasts.
Millenáris Cycle Track, Stefánia út 2. Tel: 251–1222. Trams 44, 67. Bus 7.

FOOTBALL
International matches are held in the Népstadion (Istvánmezei út 3–7, tel: 251–1222), which holds 76,000 spectators. The two leading Budapest teams are Ferencvárosi Torna Club (FTC), whose ground is at Üllői út 129 (tel: 215–6025; metro to Népliget), and Kispest-Honvéd (Új temető út 1–3; tel: 282–9789; tram 42 from the metro stop at Határ út). Matches are played at

weekends and on Wednesday evenings. Information from the monthly *Programme* obtainable at Tourinform, Sütő utca 2, tel: 117–9800.

HORSE RACING
Flat racing (*galopp*) takes place at Kincsem Park, Albertirsai út 2 (tel: 263–7950; metro to Pillangó utca) on Sundays between March and November. Trotting races (*ügető*) take place at Ügetőpálya, Kerepesi út 9 (tel: 134–2958; bus 95; trolley bus 80 from Keleti pályaudvar) at 2pm on Saturdays, 4pm on Wednesdays. Details in *Programme*. Punters may place bets at the tote.

HUNGARIAN GRAND PRIX
The Grand Prix is held annually in early August at the Mogyoród circuit, 24km northeast of Budapest (reached by car on the M3 motorway). Tourinform and English language newspapers carry details.

SPORTS FACILITIES
AEROBICS
Andi Studio
Hold utca 29. Tel: 302–4004.
Astoria Fitness Centre
Károly körút 4. Tel: 317–0452.

BOWLING
Strike Bowling Club
Budafoki út 111–113. Tel: 206–2574.

This way to the swimming bath

Vilati Bowling Club
Váci út 178. Tel: 465–1155.

CYCLING
Hungarian roads are dangerous for cyclists, but efforts are being made to create cycle paths. Tourinform should have a map of routes (*Budapest Kerékpárútjai*). Bicycle shops include Bike Cserny Shop and Service (Zuhatag sor 12, tel: 200–6837) and Rokon Bicycle (Mátyás Kitály út 6, tel: 250–3038).

FISHING
Not allowed between 20 April and 20 May. The Danube and Tisza hold carp, pike and many other species. Contact MOHOSZ (Hungarian Fishing Association, Korompai utca 17; tel: 319–9790) for information and permits. Daily tickets are available.

GOLF
Budapest Golfpark és Country Club Bt is on Szentendre Island. For details contact the city office: Bécsi utca 5. Tel: 317–6025.

HORSEBACK RIDING
Apajpuszta Hotel
Trail riding and an indoor school.
Apaj, south of Budapest. Tel: 06/24/30275.
Budapesti Lovas Klub
In the city; has a huge hall for winter exercise.
Kerepesi út 7. Tel: 313–5210.
Petneházy Country Club
Riding in the hills. Lessons available for all levels.
Feketefej utca 2–4. Tel: 397–1208.

RUNNING
The Budapest Marathon is usually held in the spring over a route between Népstadion and Római fürdő.

Enthusiastic future stars

Registration at IBUSZ on Ferenciek tere.

SWIMMING
The choice is enormous. Sports pools include:
Hajós Alfréd Nemzeti Sportuszoda (Alfréd Hajós Sport Pool)
Margitsziget. Tel: 340–4946. Open: Monday to Friday 6am–6pm, weekends 6am–2pm. (Competitions may restrict public use.)
Nyéki Imre Uszoda (Imre Nyéki Swimming Pool)
Large 33m, 8-lane pool; 27°C.
Kondorosi út 14. Tel: 208–4025. Open: Monday to Friday 6am–8pm, weekends 6am–5pm.
(See also pages 32–3.)

SQUASH
City Squash Club
Four courts. Also tennis, sauna, snooker.
Marczibányi tér 13. Tel: 212–3110. Open: 7am–midnight. Metro to Moszkva tér.

TENNIS
There are over 30 tennis clubs, but many are a long way out. It may be easier to opt for a hotel court. Try:
Flamenco Hotel – *Tas vezér utca 7. Tel: 372–2000.*
Grand Hotel Hungaria – *Rákóczi út 90. Tel: 322–9050.*
Tusculanum Hotel – *Záhony utca 10. Tel: 388–7673.*

DOG DAYS IN BUDAPEST

Non-experts could be forgiven for looking blank at the mention of an *agár*, a *puli*, a *pumi* or a *mudi*. All of them are high-performance canines bred by a people with a passion for working dogs.

The classic Hungarian breeds are believed to have accompanied the seven Magyar tribes across the Carpathians 1,100 years ago. Of these, the shaggy black *puli*, which looks like an animated hearthrug, is something of a national symbol. It is still unrivalled for rounding up sheep at pasture. Something bigger was needed to keep predators at bay, and this task was performed by the bulky *komondors* and

kuvasz (easily distinguishable from wolves and other marauders by their white colour). The beautiful *vizsla*, a ginger-coloured retriever, was kept by the Árpád kings as early as the 11th century, and the greyhound-like *agár* (also of Asian origin) was used for deer-hunting by the nobility.

Dog-fanciers can now spot (or buy) Hungarian and other breeds at the twice-yearly dog sale on Marczibányi tér. In the early days of Communism luxury breeds were virtually banned, and vets would only attend working animals. Now dogs are once again a status symbol – and often a protection against burglars.

'The more I see of men, the more I admire dogs.'

Eating Out in Budapest

*A*s in other cities of the former Eastern Bloc, the catering business enjoyed a boom following the collapse of Communism. New restaurants have mushroomed, old-established ones have been given a face-lift. Foreign investment has affected every area, but fast food, beer cellars and the luxury end of the market have benefited especially from new capital.

The better class restaurants should be booked in advance, at least for an evening. Bear in mind that you will need a taxi for reaching some of the attractive restaurants in outlying areas like the Buda Hills – it is forbidden to drive in Hungary with any alcohol in the blood.

TYPES OF EATING HOUSE

There are three main categories of eating house: an *étterem* offers a large selection of dishes and can be any price category; a *vendéglő* should offer something more like home cooking with fewer dishes to choose from, and also tends to have more ambience. *Vendéglő* prices used to be more moderate, but many have been subjected to the same sort of gentrification as similar establishments in other countries, which invariably means higher prices. A *csárda* is a country-style inn with a relatively restricted menu and simple fare. Smaller establishments with cheaper prices are called *bisztró* or, if self-service, *önkiszolgáló* or *ételbár*. A *söröző* is a beer cellar, which usually serves (fairly basic) food; a few are like ordinary restaurants.

MENU READER				
Előetelek	**(hors d'oeuvres)**		**Frissensültek**	
gombafejek rántva	fried mushrooms		**(dishes prepared to order)**	
hortobágyi			**Halételek**	(fish)
palacsinta	meat pancake with		**Balatoni fogas**	Balaton pike-perch
	sour cream		csuka	pike
libamáj	goose liver		ponty rántva	fried carp
			süllő	young pike-perch
Levesek	**(soups)**			
bableves	bean soup		**Húsételek (meat)**	
gulyásleves	goulash soup		fatányéros	mixed grill
halászlé	fishermen's broth		magyaros tál	fried meat and
meggyleves	sour cherry soup			vegetables
			sertésmáj	pig's liver
Készételek	**(ready dishes)**			
borjú pörkölt	veal stew		**Szárnyasok (poultry)**	
sertés pörkölt	pork stew		kacsa	duck
töltött káposzta	stuffed cabbage		liba	goose
töltött paprika	stuffed pepper		paprikás csirke	paprika chicken

Vadak/Vadmadarak	**(game)**
fácán	pheasant
fogoly	partridge
nyúl	hare
őzhús/szarvashús	venison
vaddisznó	wild boar
vadkacsa	wild duck
vadliba	wild goose
Tészták	**(pasta/rice)**
galuska	small dumplings
káposztás kocka	pasta with cabbage
rizs	rice
tarhonya	pasta grains
túrós csusza	pasta layers with cottage cheese
Gombócok	**(dumplings)**
barackos gombóc	apricot dumpling
szilvás gombóc	plum dumpling
Főzelék	**(vegetables)**
burgonya	potato
hasábburgonya	French fries
főtt krumpli	boiled potatoes
sült krumpli	roast potatoes
fokhagyma	garlic
hagyma	onion
káposzta	cabbage
zöldbabfőzelék	French beans
zöldpaprika	green pepper
Saláták	**(salads)**
fejes saláta	lettuce
káposztasaláta	cabbage salad
paradicsom	tomato
savanyúság	pickles
uborkasaláta	cucumber salad
(vizes) uborka	gherkin
Édességek	**(desserts)**
fagylalt	ice-cream
gesztenye püré	chestnut purée

'Gundel' palacsinta	pancake with chocolate sauce and ground walnuts
Gyümölcsök	**(fruit)**
alma	apple
banán	banana
citrom	lemon
cseresznye	cherry
meggy	Morello cherry
eper	strawberry
körte	pear
málna	raspberry
narancs	orange
őszibarack	peach
(sárga) barack	apricot
szilva	plum
Italok	**(drinks)**
fehér bor	white wine
vörös bor	red wine
édes	sweet
száraz	dry
pezsgő	'champagne' (usually Sekt)
likőr	liqueur
pálinka	
schnapps	(fruit-based)
csapolt sör	draught beer
dobozos sör	canned beer
üveges sör	bottled beer
üdítők	soft drinks
ásványvíz	still mineral water
kristályvíz	sparkling mineral water
szódavíz	soda water
jég	ice
gyümölcslé	fruit juice
kávé	coffee
tea citrommal	tea with lemon
tejes tea	tea with milk

Hungarian Cuisine

*M*ost people's idea of Hungarian cooking begins and ends with 'goulash', a dish that in Hungary itself bears little resemblance to the anaemic version served elsewhere. We think of it as a stew, but it is just as likely to be encountered as a rich meaty soup (*gulyásleves*). The origins of *gulyáshús* lie in the nomadic period of the Magyars; their horsemen would often travel for days in hostile terrain carrying iron rations of stewed mutton or beef, dried and preserved in a bag made from a sheep's stomach. To prepare a meal they would simply soften the meat in boiling water, creating a sort of instant stew. It is believed that this contributed to the success of their campaigns – the enemy had to waste time killing and cooking their food.

There is a great deal more to Hungarian cuisine than 'goulash', however. Hungary's geographical position ensured that surrounding cultures had an impact on its cooking: Balkan influence is seen in the stuffed vegetables; the sausage culture (although very ancient) has been modified by German and Italian practices; and dumplings were borrowed from the Slavs. The lands of historic Hungary had their own regional dishes, such as tarragon lamb stew from Transylvania and *lecsó* (peppers and tomatoes stewed in lard) from southern Hungary.

Fresh and conserved Hungarian produce
is first rate

The basis of most Hungarian food preparation is a heavy roux of pork lard and flour, known as *rántás*, liberally spiced, usually with paprika. Many dishes include sour cream or slices of smoked sausage, thus creating the characteristic combination of astringent and smoky tastes.

Pork (*sertés*) is the most frequent meat on the menu, usually in some kind of *pörkölt* (stew). Beef (*marha*) is not common and is seldom good quality, with one striking exception: Budapestians are fanatic consumers of steak Tartar, and many restaurants serve it with all the trappings. Lamb (*bárány*, *birka*) is hard to come by – you are more likely to encounter it in country inns.

Soups (*leves*) play a major role in Hungarian cooking. In summer an excellent cold sour cherry soup (*meggyleves*) is often on offer, while fish restaurants serve a fish soup (*halászlé*), the speciality of Szeged in southern Hungary. Freshwater fish (carp, pike, perch) from the Danube, the Tisza and Lake Balaton can be good, although it is best to order a fillet if you dislike coping with bones. The best fish is undoubtedly *fogas* (pike-perch): the Gundel chef serves it with cream cheese sauce on a bed of spinach, when it is well-nigh irresistible. More mundane are the meat and poultry dishes fried in breadcrumbs (*rántott hús*, *rántott csirke*), like a Wiener Schnitzel. Chicken paprika (*paprikás csirke*), prepared with paprika spice and sour cream, provides the tongue-tingling flavours the Magyars love. Vegetables come either stuffed (*töltött*), like cabbage or peppers, or in a *főzelék*, a delicious semi-purée (the one made with marrow – *tökfőzelék* – is especially good).

The choice of puddings tends to be rather limited, perhaps because Hungarians with a sweet tooth are well catered for by pastry shops and cafés; however, pancakes (especially the version stuffed with curds – *túró*) are a nice way to round off a meal. A sponge confection with chocolate sauce and whipped cream (*somlói galuska*) is held in affection by the locals.

Dried paprika and garlic

BARONESS ORCZY

Baroness Orczy, famed authoress of *The Scarlet Pimpernel* (1905), lived much of her life in England, although she was of Hungarian origin. Asked to compare the life-style of the two countries, she replied: 'I would say the Englishman lives like a king and eats like a pig; and the Hungarian lives like a pig, but God knows he eats like a king!'

Restaurants

Prices for all restaurants are quoted in four categories which should be taken as guidelines rather than exact figures. Average meal prices per head are implied, exclusive of drink and service (customarily 10 per cent). Service is not included unless stated on the menu-card. Inflation in Hungary is around 14 per cent, so expect price rises.

F – up to 500 Ft (fast food, snack bars, etc)
FF – up to 1,000 Ft
FFF – up to 2,000 Ft
FFFF – over 2,000 Ft

Inside a cellar restaurant

HUNGARIAN

Apostolok FFF
Marvellous 1920s interior invoking the shades of historic Hungary. Excellent service and traditional Hungarian dishes.
Kigyó utca 4–6. Tel: 267–0290. Open: daily 10am–midnight. Metro to Ferenciek tere.

Aranyszarvas FFFF
A famous game restaurant in a neo-classical house in the Tabán. Mouth-watering wild boar stew and pheasant. Reasonably restrained gypsy band.
Szarvas tér 1. Tel: 175–6451. Open: daily 6pm–midnight. Buses 5, 85 to Szarvas tér.

Bagolyvár FFF
Part of the Gundel empire (see below), but much cheaper. It concentrates on a few traditional dishes changed on a daily basis.
Állatkerti út 2. Tel: 343–0217 (Gundel's number – ask for extension 22, Bagolyvár). Open: daily noon–10pm. Metro to Hősök tere.

Csarnok Vendéglő FF
A very popular, typical Hungarian eating place with outside seating in summer.
Hold utca 11. Tel: 269–4906. Bus 70, 78 to Hold utca.

Csendes FF
Friendly service, good value. Transylvanian specialities. Ideal for lunch.
Múzeum körút 14. Tel: 267–0218. Open: Monday to Saturday noon–midnight. Metro to Astoria.

Gundel FFFF
Recently refurbished by the legendary New York restaurateur of Hungarian origin, George Lang, this has regained its former *belle époque* glory. Hungarian *haute cuisine* in elegant surroundings.

In summer Budapestians prefer to eat *al fresco*

Reservations essential.
Állatkerti út 2. Tel: 321–3550. Open: daily noon–3pm, 7pm–midnight. Metro to Hősök tere.

Kéhli Vendéglő FFF
Really excellent Hungarian cooking; aficionados rave about the bone marrow served in a red pot.
Mókus utca 22 (Óbuda). Tel: 250–4241 Open: daily 6pm–midnight. Near the Aquincum Hotel.

Kispipa Vendéglő FFF
Famous for its incredibly long and illegible menu. Inter-war ambience, old-fashioned service. Reservations recommended.
Akácfa utca 38. Tel: 324–3969. Open: Monday to Saturday noon–1am. Trams 4,6 to Wesselényi utca.

Mátyás Pince FFFF
Excellent fish and poultry; very popular with tourists. The best-known gypsy band plays here. Reservations essential.
Március 15 tér 7. Tel: 267–0264. Open: daily 11am–1am. Metro to Ferenciek tere.

Náncsi Néni Vendéglője FFF
Attractive outdoor location. Rather heavy food but some unusual specialities, eg cottage cheese dumplings.
Ördögárok utca 80. Tel: 397–2742. Open: daily noon–11pm. Far out in Hűvösvölgy – take a taxi.

Pest-Buda FFFF
A romantic location in a historic house on Castle Hill. Traditional dishes and piano music in the evening.
Fortuna utca 3. Tel: 156–9849. Open: daily noon–4am. Várbusz to Szentháromság tér.

Sipos Halászkert FFF
If you want to try fishermen's broth (*halászlé*), pike-perch (*fogas*) or carp (*ponty*), this could be the place for you. Balaton white wines to wash it down.
Fő tér 6 (Óbuda). Tel: 388–8745. Open: daily noon–midnight. HÉV to Árpád híd.

Tabáni Kakas Vendéglő FFF
The chef stresses that almost all dishes are cooked with goose fat not lard. The chicken casserole is much praised.
Attila út 27. Tel: 375–7165. Open: daily noon–midnight. Buses 5, 85 to Szarvas tér.

Tüköry Söröző FF
A place for steak Tartar buffs. Home cooking, friendly service, engagingly shabby décor.
Hold utca 15. Tel: 269–5027. Open: Monday to Friday 10am–midnight. Metro to Arany János utca.

PAPRIKA AND PALINKA

The Hungarian temperament is often said to be ardent and volatile, qualities that are mirrored in the national taste for hot spice (*paprika*) and fiery spirits (*pálinka*). The most famous of the firewaters is apricot schnapps (*Barackpálinka*), the best of which is distilled on the Alföld (Great Hungarian Plain) at Kecskemét. It is made from two varieties of apricot, the *kajszi* and the more juicy *rakovsky*, which has a strong aroma. The crushed stones of the apricots are added to the juice, and the liquid is fermented in oak barrels for at least a year. The best *barack* is sold in bottles with a white label featuring a picture of the Kecskemét town hall. Some *barack* comes in traditional long-necked flasks known as 'whistlers' (*fütyülő*) or in a *kulacs* made of Herend porcelain. The Hungarian custom is to down your *pálinka* in one gulp, which can be disconcerting, especially as it is usually drunk on an empty stomach as an aperitif.

Paprika, or capsicum, was probably introduced into Hungary in the 16th century by the Bulgarian retainers of the Turks (Bulgarians were traditionally great horticulturists). The poorer classes began using it as a condiment, a habit that spread to the nobility in the 19th century. The great Hungarian biochemist, Albert Szent-Györgyi, stumbled on capsicum's curative properties by accident, when working at Szeged University. He

Net wt. 100 g ab 3,5 oz.

mester

mester

The red pepper ("paprika")
originating from America appeared in Hungary
in the 17th century, and found a real home in sunny
Hungarian lowlands (puszta). The powder of
paprika found in the pack is hand sorted,
solar energy dried with less use of
machinery, and contains all the
natural active properties.

Hungarian
Paprika

Delicacy

The powder of paprika
is not just a coloring and seasoning
agent used for special dishes, but a rich source

... without which no
Hungarian meal is complete

but the best is said to
come from Szeged and
Kalocsa in the south. In
this region you can see
the decorative strings of
paprika pods hung out to
dry on the verandas of peasant houses.
There are several different types: a
small and hot red one, a large sweeter
red version, a green one and the
succulent yellow, ideal for eating raw
with salami. Almost all typically
Hungarian soups and main dishes are
spiced with paprika.

hated paprika, but his wife was
convinced it was good for him and
packed some in his luncheon box every
day. Unable to eat it, he decided instead
to see what it contained; his analysis led
him to the discovery of Vitamin C – and
a Nobel Prize.

    Paprika is grown all over Hungary,

Chinese restaurant

INTERNATIONAL/CONTINENTAL CUISINE
Légrádi Tsetvérek FFFF
Exclusive and intimate, with classy décor. International cuisine with a French flavour and some Hungarian dishes. Reservation essential.
Magyar utca 23. Tel: 318–6804. Open: Monday to Friday 6pm–midnight. Metro to Astoria.
The above is the Légrádi Brothers' restaurant. Irén Légrádi has opened an equally stylish establishment at nearby *Bárczy István utca 3–5, tel: 266–4993.*
Robinson FFFF
Attractively located on a raft on the lake of Városliget (City Woodland Park). Carefully chosen menu of international and Hungarian dishes. Guitar music.
Városligeti tó, Állatkerti körút 1. Tel: 343–3776. Open: daily noon–3.30pm, 6.30–11pm (weekends dinner only). Metro to Hősök tere.

Seefisch/Tengerihal FF
Good quality seafood.
Múzeum körút 5. Tel: 266–6633. Open: Monday to Friday 9am–9pm, Saturday 10am–9pm. Metro to Kálvin tér.
Vadrózsa FFFF
The most fashionable restaurant in town, situated in a baroque villa on the Rózsadomb. Extremely expensive set price meal, no menu and no wine list (the waiter advises). Terrace in summer.
Pentelei Molnár utca 15. Tel: 326–5817. Open: Tuesday to Sunday 6pm–midnight. Bus 91 to Vérhalom tér, or take a taxi.

AMERICAN
Chicago Restaurant FF
Ribs, burgers and drinkable draught beer. Very friendly service.
Erzsébet körút 2. Tel: 269–6753. Open: daily noon–midnight. Metro to Blaha Lujza tér.
Rolling Rock Café FF
American-style eatery with American and Mexican fare.
Bécsi út 53–55. Tel: 368–2298. Tram 17 to Kolosy tér.

CHINESE
Great Wall FFF
Cantonese cuisine.
Ajtósi Dürer sor 1. Tel: 343–8895. Open: daily 11.30am–11.30pm. Trolley buses 75, 79 to Ajtósi Dürer sor.
Taiwan FFF
Critics' choice for good quality Chinese food. Long menu.
Gyáli út 3b. Tel: 215–1236. Open: daily noon–midnight. Metro to Nagyvarád tér.

CZECH
Prágai Wencel Sörház FFF
Czech specialities, draught Pilsener Urquell.
Rákóczi út 57. Tel: 333–1342. Open: daily 11am–midnight. Metro to Blaha Lujza tér.

Svejk FFF
Cheerful atmosphere; big portions of Czech and Slovak specialities. Handy for the Music Academy.
Király utca 59b. Tel: 322–3278. Open: daily noon–11pm. Trams 4, 6 to Király utca.

FRENCH
Le Jardin de Paris FFFF
Bistro-style atmospheric restaurant with French wines on offer – at a price. Late-night opening with live jazz in the evenings.
Fő utca 20. Tel: 201–0047. Open: daily 11am–2am. Metro to Batthyány tér.

GREEK
Jorgosz Greek Taverna FFF
Authentic décor, music and food in a Pest cellar.
Csengery utca 24. Tel: 341–0772. Open: daily noon–2am. Metro to Vörösmarty utca.

ITALIAN
Kis Itália FF
Excellent pizzas and pasta; good service.
Szemere utca 22. Tel: 269–3145. Open: Monday to Saturday 11am–9pm. Metro to Kossuth Lajos tér.
Marco Polo FFFF
Claimed by some to offer the best food (of any kind) in the city. Prices match the claim.
Vigadó tér 3. Tel: 138–3925. Open: daily noon–3pm, 7.30pm–midnight. Tram 2 to Vigadó tér.

JAPANESE
Japán Étterem FFFF
Worth a visit for the prawns and lobsters – if money is no object.
Luther utca 4–6. Tel: 314–3427. Open: Monday to Saturday noon–2pm, 6–11pm.

Metro to Blaha Lujza tér.

JEWISH
Carmel Pince FFF
Kosher specialities in pleasant surroundings. Very popular, so reserve.
Kazinczy utca 31. Tel: 322–1834. Open: daily noon–11pm. Metro to Astoria.

KOREAN
Senara Korean Restaurant FFF
The cheaper of Budapest's two Korean restaurants, but just as authentic.
Dohány utca 5. Tel: 352–6549.Open: daily 11.30am–2.30pm, 6–11pm. Metro to Astoria.

VEGETARIAN
Vegetárium FFF
All there is for vegetarians in the city, apart from salad bars. Has a good reputation among the *cognoscenti.*
Cukor utca 3. Tel: 267–0322. Open: daily noon–10pm. Metro to Ferenciek tere.

Pizzas have arrived in a big way

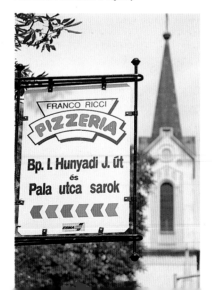

Food and Drink

SÖRÖZOK (Beer Halls)

Budapest beer cannot compare with Czech or German brews, which are luckily increasingly available in the capital. Austrian beer (particularly the ubiquitous Gösser) is also common, due to heavy Austrian investment in Hungarian breweries.

Ádám Söröző FF

Traditional beer hall serving Staropramen Prague beer. Very good value and friendly service.
Andrássy út 41. Tel: 352–1338. Open: daily 9am–11pm. Metro to Opera.

Becketts Irish Bar FF

Authentic Irish pub with live entertainment. Voted best pub *and* best entertainment (1995–6).
Bajcsy–Zsilinszky út 72. Tel: 311–1003. Open: noon–1am. Metro to Bajcsy–Zsilinszky út.

John Bull Pub FFF

English beer and food, but expensive and only for those who cannot survive without their pint....
Apáczai Csere János utca 17. Tel: 318–6847. Open: daily noon–midnight. Tram 2 to Eötrös tér.

Pilsner Urquell FFF

Prices reflect Váci utca location, but it is handy for a shopper's lunch.
Váci utca 15. Tel: 118–3814. Open: daily 10am–11pm. Metro to Ferenciek tere.

Söröző a Szent Jupáthoz FF

Beer cellar offering figure-destroying fare round the clock.
Retek utca 16. Tel: 212–2923. Open: 24 hours. Metro to Moszkva tér.

KÁVÉZÓK, CUKRÁSZDÁK
(Cafés, cake shops)

Some coffee houses miraculously survived the kill-joy ethos of Communism and are now recapturing the spirit of a more leisured age.

Angelika F

A favourite meeting place on the Buda side, cosy in winter, cool in summer on the terrace.
Batthyány tér 7. Tel: 212–3784. Open: daily 10am–10pm. Metro to Batthyány tér.

Gerbeaud FF

The most famous of Pest's cafés since Swiss patissier, Emil Gerbeaud, took it over in 1883. Period interior, excellent pastries (which you can also take away).
Vörösmarty tér 7. Tel: 118–1311. Open: daily 9am–9pm. Metro to Vörösmarty tér.

Lukács F

Said to have the best pastries in town. Nostalgic atmosphere and décor.

Inside the New York café

Beer halls are good value and the choice of foreign beer is increasing all the time

Andrássy út 79. Tel: 302–8747. Open:
daily 9am–8pm. Metro to Oktogon.
Művész F
Delightful turn-of-the-century interior.
Usually full of musicians and artistes.
Andrássy út 29. Tel: 267–0689. Open:
Monday to Saturday 8am–10pm. Metro to
Opera.
New York FF
The playwright Ferenc Molnár
celebrated the opening of Café New
York in 1896 by throwing its door-key
into the Danube, so that it should
remain open night and day. It was the
haunt of journalists, writers and actors at
the turn of the century, but is now very
touristy with prices to match. Worth a
visit to see the interior.
Erzsébet körút 9–11. Tel: 322–3849.
Open: daily 9am–10pm. Metro to Blaha
Lujza tér.
Ruszwurm F
Minute and charming café with original
Biedermeier cherry-wood furnishings.
The cream slice (krémes) is the best in
town.

Szentháromság utca 7. Tel: 175–5284.
Open: Thursday to Tuesday 10am–8pm.
Várbusz to Szentháromság tér.

FAST FOOD
The range has expanded enormously in
recent years. The following are reliable:

Jégbüfé Cukrászda FF
Very convenient for that fresh pastry and
quick coffee.
Ferenciek tere 10. Tel: 267–3275. Open:
8am–6pm. Metro to Ferenciek tére.
McDonald's F
The one at the Western Railway Station
(Nyugati pályaudvar) has a classic
interior; convenient are those in
Régiposta utca (just off Váci utca) and
Süto utca (next to Tourinform).
Open: 9am–10pm.
New York Bagel
The real thing! Delivery service
available.
Bajcsy–Zsilinszky út 21. Tel: 311–8441.
Open 24 hours. Metro to Deák tér.

WINES OF HUNGARY

To wine buffs familiar only with the much-promoted *Egri Bikaver* (Bulls' Blood from Eger), Hungarian viticulture offers the prospect of interesting discoveries. The country has 16 wine-growing regions producing many refreshing and somewhat acidic white wines, together with a number of full-bodied reds. Most Hungarian wine is drunk young, and over-production of poor quality plonk is endemic, made worse by the collapse of the huge Russian market. (Asked why he did not export the resultant surplus elsewhere, one producer gravely replied:

'Because it is unfit for human consumption.')

To learn about the better quality wines one could do worse than visit the Magyar Borok Háza (House of Hungarian wines) where there is a choice of 420 wines from all regions and tasting is possible (Szentháromság tér 6, Castle Hill, tel: 212–1030; open 11am–7pm).

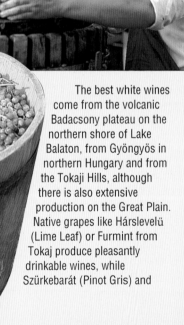

The best white wines come from the volcanic Badacsony plateau on the northern shore of Lake Balaton, from Gyöngyös in northern Hungary and from the Tokaji Hills, although there is also extensive production on the Great Plain. Native grapes like Hárslevelű (Lime Leaf) or Furmint from Tokaj produce pleasantly drinkable wines, while Szürkebarát (Pinot Gris) and

After years of quantity determined production, some Hungarian suppliers are now turning back to quality

Olaszrizsling (Italian Riesling) are good Balaton products. The best reds come from the Villány region of southern Hungary, whose Cabernet Sauvignons and Merlots are occasionally outstanding.

Uniquely Hungarian is the famous golden dessert wine, Tokaji Aszú – 'the wine of kings and king of wines'. The region in northeastern Hungary where it is produced has undergone upheaval because of privatisation and ownership disputes, but the honeyed nectar is still available. Once you have tried it you will understand the enthusiasm of Pope Benedict who wrote to thank Maria Theresa for a consignment in the 18th century and delivered a graceful eulogy of Tokaji: 'Blessed is the land that produced you, blessed the lady who sent you; and blessed am I who drink you.'

Hotels and Accommodation

*B*udapest is exceptional in having tackled the shortage of hotel accommodation much sooner than other former Eastern Bloc capitals. The 55,000 beds of 1989 have been considerably added to and new hotels are still opening, albeit at a slower rate. These must cater for a throughput of around five million visitors annually. Availability can be strained at peak times (mid-summer, when the Grand Prix is held, Christmas and New Year).

Those who can be more flexible than businessmen in a hurry should have little problem finding accommodation, providing they are happy to consider staying in the private rooms that double the bed supply at peak periods. For hotels it is vital to book in advance from abroad if you want a specific location or facility (eg a Danube view or a quiet room not overlooking a main thoroughfare). You should bear in mind that mid-price hotels may have taken block bookings from tour operators up to a year in advance; there remains a shortage of this sort of accommodation because of the obsession of developers with profitable luxury hotels.

PRICES

As elsewhere in Eastern Europe the standards prevailing in any given star category may not always match up to the expectations of western visitors, though this mostly applies to older establishments in the upper mid-price bracket. Even then there may be compensations (for instance, the Gellért's wonderful spa makes up for its less pleasing bedrooms). The newly built hotels all meet the highest European standards (the 5-star Grand Hotel Corvinus Kempinski, opened in 1992, and the delightful Thermal Aquincum in Old Buda, for example). The long-established waterfront hotels in Pest also maintain a high level of service; one of them (the Duna Intercontinental) has been acquired by Marriott Hotels, who have refurbished it.

The following price structure indicates what one might expect to pay for a double room with breakfast in different categories of accommodation in Budapest. Inflation is running at around 14 per cent, but the luxury hotels adjust their prices more in line with international norms.

5-star – 25,000 Ft or above
4-star – 12,000 to 25,000 Ft
3-star – 8,000 to 12,000 Ft
2-star – 6,000 to 8,000 Ft
Cheaper hotels: 4,000 to 6,000 Ft.
The cost of a private room may be cheaper still – it should be possible to find a pleasant room at around 3,000 Ft (probably not including breakfast) and something acceptable for a bit less.

LOCATION

The decision where to stay in the city is likely to be determined by convenience and aesthetics in that order. If you stay in the Buda Hills (for example in the Hotel Olympia at Normafa) the air is good, but you have a longish trek into the city. Castle Hill has the best of all worlds – a lovely situation, cleaner air and rapid access to the centre: unfortunately, your choice here is limited to the relatively

The old and the new: the distinguished spa hotel, the Gellért and the luxurious Grand Hotel Corvinus Kempinski

expensive Hilton. There are some cheaper hotels in the Víziváros below Castle Hill on the Buda side and one botel moored not far from Batthyány tér (Dunapart Hotel, Szilágyi Dezső tér).

On the Pest side there are two hotels with classic waterfront locations (the Fórum-Intercontinental and the Marriott) and one within spitting distance of the river (Átrium Hyatt).

Otherwise your choice is mostly from hotels in the densely built heart of Pest or along the boulevards. In addition there are several good hotels beyond or around the Tabán/Gellért Hill area (Victoria, Orion, Flamenco and Gellért).

The lobby of the superbly located Hilton Hotel on Castle Hill

BOOKING AGENCIES (hotels, private rooms, apartments)

In the season you may well be greeted at the railway termini and outside booking agencies by private individuals with rooms to let. If you prefer a more formal arrangement, there are various agencies that will help you find the sort of accommodation you require. If you want a private room, look for the desk marked *fizetővendég* (paying guest service). In such accommodation bathroom and kitchen facilities may have to be shared, and a stay of less than four days attracts a supplement of 30 per cent.

Budapest Tourist

Over 5,000 rooms available.
This agency has several branches and also organises tours of the city and some of the most attractive excursions. Its main branch is at Roosevelt tér 5 (tel: 118–1658). Open Monday to Friday 8am–8pm, 9am–noon at weekends. Another branch is at Baross tér 3, near the Eastern Railway Station.

Cooptourist

About 2,500 rooms available. The most convenient branch is at Bajcsy-Zsilinszky út 17 (tel: 331–0992); open: Monday to Saturday 8am–5pm.

IBUSZ

3,000 rooms available.
Oktogon 3 (tel: 322–4234), Erzsébet körút (tel: 322–7467), Vörosmarty tér 5 (tel: 317–2322); all open daily 8am–8pm. József Attila utca 18 (tel: 118–6228); open: 8am–5pm, Saturday and Sunday 8am–noon.

IBUSZ Hotel and Room Service,

IBUSZ has an office open 12 hours a day at Apáczai Csene János utca 1 (tel: 118–4848 for bookings).

HOTELS
Luxury hotels

The last word in luxury is the **Grand Hotel Corvinus Kempinski** (tel: 266–1000), in a class of its own for facilities and opulence.

However, the **Hilton** (tel: 214–1000) has a superb view and good location in the old town of Buda. The three river-front hotels – **Budapest Marriott** (formerly Duna Intercontinental, tel: 266–7000), **Fórum** (tel: 327–6333) and **Átrium-Hyatt** (tel: 266–1234) – offer fine views of the Royal Palace and Castle Hill.

Mid-range hotels

Traditional hotels that have been given a face-lift include the **Nemzeti** (tel: 303–9340) and the **Béke Radisson** (tel: 301–1600). Two rather soulless products of the '60s and '70s, which nevertheless have plenty of facilities, are **Novotel** (tel: 209–1980), and **Flamenco** (tel: 372–2000). The **Erzsébet** (tel: 328–5700) is pleasant and centrally located.

Two places with character are the old **Astoria** (tel: 317–3411), refurbished but retaining its traditional ambience, and the new **Korona** (tel: 117–4111) a post-modern building near the Magyar Nemzeti Múzeum (National Museum).

Thermal hotels

A speciality of Budapest is the spa hotel, of which the **Gellért** (tel: 385–2200) is the most distinguished. There are two spa hotels on the lovely Margaret Island: the **Thermal** (tel: 329–2300) and the **Ramada Grand Hotel** (tel: 329–2300), the latter in a restored building designed by Miklós Ybl. An attractive addition to the hotel scene is the **Hotel Thermal Aquincum** in Óbuda (tel: 436–4100).

Smaller hotels and pensions

If you want a hotel that is different (but spartan), the **Citadella** (tel: 466–5794) on the summit of Gellért Hill has 11 rooms. The **Panoráma** (tel: 395–6121) has a nice situation at the end of the cogwheel railway. Many pensions are also quite a long way out, but they are almost always homely and pleasant.

Youth hostels

To book a youth hostel go with your membership card to **Expressz Központi Iroda**, Szabadság tér 16, tel: 131–7777. They also have an office at Keleti pályaudvar (Eastern Railway Station).

Hotel Thermal Aquincum

On Business

*H*ungary's transformation from command economy to free market was assisted by the tentative opening to private enterprise under the Communists. Privatisation of profitable or promising concerns happened quickly, but the second stage of restructuring is more painful. Recession has choked off some potential investors, and the unattractiveness of many of the ailing businesses on offer has deterred others. Against this, the increase in competitiveness, even between state sector concerns, is palpable, and many Hungarian businessmen have coped well with the collapse of traditional COMECON markets and the switch to hard currency contracts.

As a small land-locked country without significant natural resources, Hungary is heavily dependent on foreign trade – nearly 50 per cent of GDP is exported. Tourism is a major source of hard currency.

BUSINESS ACCOMMODATION AND TRAVEL
American Express
(Deák Ferenc utca 10; tel: 235–4330) serves the requirements of visiting businessmen.

All 5-star hotels have facilities such as conference rooms, fax and secretarial services; most 4-star hotels offer some business facilities.
Estate agents (commercial property and executive location)
CD Hungary
Benczúr utca 42. Tel: 351–1777. Fax: 351–1797.
Healey & Baker
Rákóczi út 42. Tel: 268–1288.
Jones Lang Wootton
Váci utca 81. Tel: 266–4981. Fax: 266–0142.

BUSINESS HOURS
The working day is eight hours, usually from 8am to 4.30pm with a half-hour break for lunch. Industrial workers begin

and end the day earlier than office workers. For shopping hours, see the **Practical Guide**, page 188.

CONGRESSES/FAIRS
Budapest has a large congress centre, the **Budapest Kongresszusi Központ** (Jagelló út 1–3; tel: 209–4850). Information concerning the various trade fairs held during the year may be obtained from the Director of the Budapest Fairs Centre (HUNGEXPO), X Budapest, Albertirsai út 10 (postal address: H–1441 Budapest. Pf 44). Tel: 263–6000. Fax: 263–6098.

Important fairs include International Tourism (March), Agriculture (April), Information Technology (April) and Medical Equipment (October). A major innovation is the Budapest International Wine Festival (usually the second week in September), primarily a showcase for Hungarian wines.

ETIQUETTE
Hungarians are meticulous about greetings: if you meet with a delegation you will be expected to introduce yourself and shake hands with each person individually. Business cards are widely used, so take a good supply of your own. Hungarians doing a lot of business with

other countries may use the conventional name order, but most will follow the Hungarian order with surname first.

Punctuality is not a Hungarian obsession. If a business partner arrives 15 minutes late, no insult is intended. Business meetings invariably begin with ritual coffee drinking. The decision-making process is slow and the inbred instinct of functionaries to check everything with higher layers of authority is still common.

MONEY

The exchange rate is fixed daily by the National Bank of Hungary against an average of the US dollar and the ECU. The currency is convertible. Rates are posted at exchange kiosks, in banks and at American Express (Deák Ferenc utca 10, tel: 235–4330). Most banks are open from 8.30am to 3.30pm on weekdays. Exchange kiosks and travel bureaux will change money any time in working hours and (in the case of kiosks) at weekends.

SERVICES TO BUSINESSMEN
Accountancy
Dénes and Daughter Ltd
Accountancy and audit. International experience.
Berenczey utca 21. Tel/fax: 218–0416.

Office and secretarial
Irodaház Kft
City centre location. Full range of services.
Révay utca 10. Tel: 269–1100. Fax: 269–1030.
Regus Kft
The instant office provider, plus video conferencing, etc.
Rákóczi út 42. Tel: 267–9111. Fax: 267–9100.

The Congress Centre

Courier
DHL Magyarország Kft
Rákóczi út 1–3. Tel: 266–5555. Fax: 266–2640.

Customs clearance
Business Umbrella
East-West Business Centre, Rákóczi út 1–3. Tel: 269–6999.

Office supplies
Ápisz
General stationers.
Andrássy út 3 (tel: 268–0534), Margit körút 48 (tel: 201–0451).

Photocopying
Copy General
Semmelweis utca 4. Tel: 266–6564. Fax: 266–6563. Open: Monday to Friday 7am–10pm. Also at: Lónyay utca 13. Tel: 216–8880. Fax: 217–1592. Open: Monday to Friday, 24 hours.

Translation and interpreting
FORDUNA Fordító és Tolmács Bt
Multilingual translation, interpreting and certification.
Bartók Béla út 86. Tel: 209–2482. Fax: 165–9668.
Intercontact Budapest Kft
Translation, interpreting, word processing. Specialist in bank, legal and technical documents.
Bajcsy-Zsilinszky út 27. Tel: 269–1153. Fax: 312–5408.

Practical Guide

ARRIVING

Visas

Citizens of the US, Canada, South Africa, Great Britain and most countries of continental Europe need only a valid passport to enter Hungary for a stay of up to 90 days (British Visitors' Passports do not qualify).

Citizens of Australia, New Zealand and most non-European countries require a visa, obtainable at Hungarian consulates (usually within 24 hours). If you are travelling to and fro, get a multiple entry visa for 12 months.

Visas are obtainable at Ferihegy Airport and at main highway border crossings, but not on international trains. In the UK the Thomas Cook Passport and Visa Service can advise and obtain necessary documentation – ask your Thomas Cook travel consultant.

By air

Ferihegy Airport is 16km southwest of the city. **Malév** (Hungarian Airlines) operate out of Terminal 2 (tel: 296–8000); most other flights use Terminal 1 (tel: 296–7155/6000). Reasonable deals on flights from London to Budapest (eg APEX fares) can be arranged through British Airways and Malév. From the US, Malév, Delta and Lufthansa fly direct.

The best way of getting into the city is with the Airport Minibus Shuttle, which will deliver you anywhere for around 1,200 Ft. It can also pick you up from your accommodation in town to take you to the airport (tel: 296–8555).

The LRI Minibus runs between Erzsébet tér in the centre and the airport on the half hour every day between 5am and 9pm. It is cheaper, but less convenient, to take the 93 bus to Kőbánya–Kispest metro station and then the metro into town.

Try to avoid taxis from the airport: overcharging and unpleasantness are almost inevitable.

By rail

Budapest has three international train stations: Nyugati pályaudvar (Western

Airport minibus

Railway Station), Keleti pályaudvar
(Eastern Railway Station) – both in Pest
– and Déli pályaudvar (Southern
Railway Station), in Buda. There is a
direct metro link to the city centre from
all three.

The *Thomas Cook European
Timetable*, published monthly and
providing up-to-date details of most rail
services and many shipping services
throughout Europe, will help you plan a
rail journey to, from and around
Hungary. You can buy it in the UK
from some stations, any branch of
Thomas Cook or by telephoning 01733
503571.

In the USA, contact the Forsyth
Travel Library Inc, 226 Westchester
Avenue, White Plains, New York 10604,
USA. Tel: 800/367 7984.

By bus
International bus services arrive at the
Erzsébet tér bus terminal (tel: 117–2562,
6am–6pm) adjacent to Deák Ferenc tér
in Pest. All three metro lines converge at
Deák tér. There are daily buses from
Munich and Vienna to Budapest run by
the Hungarian firm of Volán and the
Austrian Blaguss line.

Eurolines (Victoria Coach Station,
London, tel: 0171 730–0202) and
Attila Tours (36A Kilburn High Road,
NW6, tel: 0171 372–0470) run a bus
service from London to Budapest in
summer.

By car
Border crossings on arterial roads are
open 24 hours, on smaller ones between
7am and midnight.

For local information

By hydrofoil
Hydrofoils run between Vienna and
Budapest from April to September.
Information in Vienna from IBUSZ
(tel: 53 2686) or the DDSG (tel: 58 88
00).

In Budapest they dock at the
MAHART landing stage of the Belgrád
rakpart on the Pest side (tel: 118–1953).
The journey takes four and a half hours.

CAMPING
Magyar Camping és Caravanning Club has reductions for FIIC members. *Üllői út 6. Tel: 133–6536. Open: Monday to Friday 8am–4pm.*

Camp sites
Hárshegyi Camping (Római part üdülőfalu Rt)
1 May to 15 October.
Hárshegyi út 5–7. Tel: 115–1482.
Expo Autocamping (International Trade Fair Site)
20 June to 5 September.
Albertirsai út 10, Gate 4. Tel: 177–8314.
Római Fürdő Camping (Aquincum)
1 May to 15 October.
Szentendrei út 189. Tel: 368–6260.

CHILDREN
Children up to six travel free on public transport. The chain store **Skála** sells baby food, nappies (*nadrág pelenka*), etc. The biggest specialist store is **ProBaby**

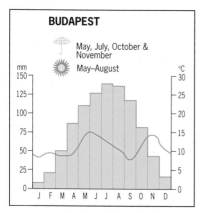

BUDAPEST

☂ May, July, October & November
☀ May–August

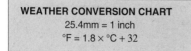

WEATHER CONVERSION CHART
25.4mm = 1 inch
°F = 1.8 × °C + 32

at Deák Ferenc utca 13 (near to Deák metro station) – tel: 117–2189.

CLIMATE
Hungary has a continental climate – very hot in mid-summer, bitterly cold in winter. Most of the weather comes from the west, but occasionally the wind blows from the Russian steppe in the northeast, bringing much severer conditions. See chart for details.

CONVERSION TABLES
See tables opposite.

CRIME
Despite an enormous increase in petty crime, Budapest is not a dangerous place. Beware of pickpockets, however, especially in the Váci utca area, and do not leave valuables in hotel rooms or cars. Car theft is a big problem. Do not change money on the black market.

The police emergency number is 107 and the Budapest police headquarters are at Teve utca 4–6 (tel: 343–0034 or 343–1034) but go first to the nearest police station.

CUSTOMS REGULATIONS
Personal effects may be brought in duty-free. Anyone over 16 may bring 250 cigarettes or 50 cigars or 250g of tobacco; also 2 litres of wine or 1 litre of spirits; and small presents up to the value of 16,000 Ft. Pornography and drugs are forbidden, as are firearms without prior authorisation.

The convertibility of the *forint* means that money may be taken in and out of the country, but large cash sums will arouse suspicions of money laundering. Antique works of art require an export certificate from the Hungarian National Gallery.

Conversion Table

FROM	TO	MULTIPLY BY
Inches	Centimetres	2.54
Feet	Metres	0.3048
Yards	Metres	0.9144
Miles	Kilometres	1.6090
Acres	Hectares	0.4047
Gallons	Litres	4.5460
Ounces	Grams	28.35
Pounds	Grams	453.6
Pounds	Kilograms	0.4536
Tons	Tonnes	1.0160

To convert back, for example from centimetres to inches, divide by the number in the third column.

Men's Suits

UK		36	38	40	42	44	46 48
Rest of Europe	46	48	50	52	54	56	58
US		36	38	40	42	44	46 48

Dress Sizes

UK	8	10	12	14	16	18
France	36	38	40	42	44	46
Italy	38	40	42	44	46	48
Rest of Europe	34	36	38	40	42	44
US	6	8	10	12	14	16

Men's Shirts

UK	14	14.5	15	15.5	16	16.5	17
Rest of Europe	36	37	38	39/40	41	42	43
US	14	14.5	15	15.5	16	16.5	17

Men's Shoes

UK	7	7.5	8.5		9.5	10.5	11
Rest of Europe	41	42	43		44	45	46
US	8	8.5	9.5		10.5	11.5	12

Women's Shoes

UK		4.5	5	5.5	6	6.5	7
Rest of Europe	38	38	39	39		40	41
US		6	6.5	7	7.5	8	8.5

The **Vám és Pénzügyőrség Információs Szogálata** (Customs Information Office) is at Falk Miksa utca 2 (tel: 311–5487; open: Monday 8am–5pm, Tuesday to Thursday 8am–3pm, Friday 8am–noon).

DISABLED TRAVELLERS

Facilities for the disabled are generally poor. However, advice and information on accommodation and specialist tours are provided by: **Egalitas Foundation**, Len utca 15/A. Tel: 176–5755. Fax: 395–0473.

DRIVING

Alcohol

There is an absolute prohibition on drinking and driving. Breathalysing is common.

Breakdown

The Hungarian Automobile Club (MAK) runs a 'Yellow Angels' (*sárga angyal*) service for motorists in distress, but it can be hard to get through to their emergency number in summer (088, 24 hours). The main office is at Rómer F utca 4/A 38A, tel: 212–2938/2821.

Reciprocal arrangements cover members of most European motoring clubs. Private breakdown services: **Americar Service** (tel: 129–9084), **Budasegély** (tel: 250–0996), **Start** (tel: 350–0899) and **Toman** (tel: 311–304).

Documents and insurance

An International Driving Licence is advisable. Motorists should bring with them the vehicle's registration document and green card insurance. It is obligatory to carry a first aid kit, a red warning triangle and replacement light bulbs. The

Major car-hire companies are represented

vehicle should display a national identification sticker.

Insurance problems and temporary cover are dealt with by **Hungária Biztosító**, Hamzsabégi út 60, tel: 209–0730, extensions 2250–54; open: Monday to Friday 8am–4pm, Friday 7.30am–3pm, Saturday 8am–noon.

Fuel

Petrol stations (*benzinkút*) sell 98 (extra), 92 (super) and 86 octane petrol. Stations on main thoroughfares and arteries also sell 95 (unleaded) and diesel, but elsewhere these may be difficult to find.

Shell, BP and Aral are well represented. Convenient 24-hour petrol stations in Budapest are at Szervita tér 8, Keleti pályaudvar (Pest), Szilágyi Erzsébet fasor 53 (Buda side) and Szentendrei út 373 (Óbuda).

Parking

In Pest you can forget about street parking. There are a few multi-storey or underground car parks in the centre (Aranykéz utca 4, Szervita tér 8). Visitors to the Forum or Kempinski hotels can use their underground car parks.

Getting towed away is a hazard for Budapest drivers. Phone 383–0700 or the police on 107 for information on your missing car. Car pounds are at Nagyszombat utca 2 (buses 6, 60, 84, 86) and Gerlóczy utca 2.

Traffic regulations

Drive on the right. Yield to traffic from the right unless you are on a priority road (marked with a yellow diamond sign). Seat belts are compulsory front and back (if fitted). Stop for passengers who alight from trams directly into the road (but you may continue if there is a passenger island at the tram stop).

Trams have the right of way, ditto buses pulling out from stops. The speed limit in built-up areas is 50kph, on minor roads 80kph, on main roads 100kph, on motorways 120kph. A 1993 regulation makes it obligatory to drive with dipped headlights outside the city in daylight hours.

Notify all accidents to the police and report damage to Hungária Biztosító (see **Documents**).

ELECTRICITY

220 volts 50 cycles AC. Standard continental adaptors are suitable. 100/120 volt appliances require a voltage transformer.

EMBASSIES

Australia: Királyhágó tér 8–9. Tel: 212–1025.

Canada: Budakeszi út 32. Tel: 275–1200.

South Africa: Rákóczi út 1–3. Tel: 267–4566/7.

UK: Harmincad utca 6. Tel: 266–2888 (10am–6pm). The UK embassy acts on behalf of New Zealand citizens.

US: Szabadság tér 12. Tel: 267–4400.

EMERGENCIES
Ambulance 104
24-hour emergency medical service
(English) tel: 311–1666.
Chemist (24-hour pharmacies)
Üllői út 121, tel: 215–3800 (Pest);
Frankel Leó út 22 (2nd district),
tel: 212–4406 (Buda side); Széna
tér 1 (1st district), tel: 202–1816 (Castle
Hill).
Dentist
SOS Dental Clinic
24-hour treatment. Language may be a
problem.
Király utca 14. Tel: 267–6710.
Doctor
There are 24-hour casualty departments
at Hold utca 19 (tel: 111–6816) and
Vihar utca 29 (8am–8pm, tel: 388–8501)
and English-speaking help on 118–8212.
Private treatment including 24-hour
emergency service from **International
Therapeutic Services Ltd** (Váci út
202, tel: 129–8423, 149–9349;
consultation hours Monday to Friday
7.30am–8pm).
Fire brigade 105
Police 107

HEALTH
No special vaccinations are needed for
Hungary, but keep tetanus and polio
immunisation up to date.

As in every other part of the world,
AIDS is present. Water is safe to drink.
Generally visitors must pay for health
care, whether state or private.

British citizens are entitled to free
emergency treatment under a reciprocal
agreement, but all visitors are advised to
have full health insurance cover.

Many doctors and dentists work
privately as well as in the state sector.
Lists of those speaking your language
may be obtained from your embassy.

The underpaid doctors, surgeons and
nurses traditionally receive a gratuity
from patients, ranging from 10,000 Ft for
an operation to at least 1,000 Ft for
nurses.

For 24-hour casualty departments see
under **Emergencies**. For non-emergency
dental treatment go to the Stomatológiai
Intézet (Central Dental Institute) of the
Szájsebészeti Klinika, Mária utca 52
(tel: 266–0457).

Broken bones are dealt with by the
Országos Traumatológiai Kórház,
Fiumei út 17 (tel: 333–7599).

HOLIDAYS
1 January (New Year's Day)
15 March (Anniversary of 1848
  revolution)
Easter Monday
1 May (Labour Day)
20 August (St Stephen's and
  Constitution Day)

Keeping up with the news

23 October (Anniversary of the 1956 revolution)
25 and 26 December (Christmas).

INSURANCE
Travel insurance is advisable. Check that the policy covers all medical treatment, loss of documents, repatriation, baggage, money and valuables.

LOST PROPERTY
BKV Talált Tárgyak Osztálya
(Lost Property Office of the Budapest Transport System), Akácfa utca 18. Tel: 322–6613. Office hours: Monday and Thursday 7.30am–3pm, Wednesday 7.30am–7pm, Friday 7.30am–2pm.

Otherwise try the police station nearest to where you lost the item. Passport loss should be reported to your embassy and to the police. Your embassy should be able to advise you what further action needs to be taken and may direct you to the Aliens Bureau at Izabella utca 61.

MAPS
Recommended are the *Budapest Atlasz* by Cartographia and the same publisher's *Belváros* (Inner City) map. Buy the current edition for up-to-date street names.

MEDIA
Local English-language newspapers are the *Budapest Week* and *The Budapest Sun* and the new glossy *Style* magazine. These and foreign publications can be bought at city-centre news-stands and larger hotels. Radio Bridge (102.1 FM) has some English programmes and American news.

MONEY MATTERS
Travellers' cheques and Eurocheques are widely accepted. In the relevant associate banks you can get cash advances on a credit card.

Banks are usually open Monday to Friday 8.30am–3.30pm.

OTP (Post Office Savings Bank) makes no charge on exchange. Exchange kiosks are heavy on charges but keep longer hours.

The Hungarian *forint* is denominated in 10,000, 5,000, 1,000, 500 and 200 notes. Coin denominations are 1, 2, 5, 10, 20, 50 and 100. The *forint* is divided into 100 (worthless) *fillér*.

Thomas Cook Travellers Cheques free you from the hazards of carrying large amounts of cash. Some hotels, restaurants and shops accept them in lieu of cash.

If you need to transfer money quickly, you can use the *MoneyGram*[SM] Money Transfer service. For more details in the UK, telephone Freephone 0800 897198.

OPENING HOURS
Food shops are open Monday to Friday 7am or 8 am to 6pm; Saturday 8am to noon or 1pm.

Other shops are open Monday to Friday 10am to 5pm or 6pm, Saturday 9am to 1pm (but some do not open on Saturday).

For museums see individual entries; for office hours see **On Business**, page 178.

POST OFFICES
The main post office (*posta*) and *poste restante* are at Városház utca 18 (tel: 318–4811), open Monday to Friday 8am–6pm, Saturday 8am–2pm; 24-hour post offices operate at Teréz körút 51 and Baross tér 11C (near Nyugati and Keleti railway stations).

LANGUAGE

Pronunciation

The stress is always on the first syllable.

Vowel sounds

a like the **o** in h**o**t
á like the **u** in h**u**t but twice as long
e as in p**e**n
é as in pl**a**y
i as in s**i**t
í as in m**ea**t
o like the **aw** in p**aw** but shorter
ó the same but longer
ö like the **ur** in f**ur**
ő the same only longer
u as in f**u**ll
ú like the **oo** in s**oo**n
ü as in German f**ü**nf
ű the same but longer

Consonants

b, d, f, h, m, n, v, x, z as in English
c like **ts** in ha**ts**
cs like **ch** in **ch**oose
g as in **g**ull
gy like the **d** in **d**uring
j/ly both like **y**
ny like the **n** in **n**ew
r rolled as in Scottish
s like **sh** in **sh**ip
sz like **s** in **s**ea
t as in si**t**
ty like the **tti** in pre**tti**er
zs like the **s** in plea**s**ure.

Numbers

1 egy		6 hat	
2 kettő		7 hét	
3 három		8 nyolc	
4 négy		9 kilenc	
5 öt		10 tíz	

Days of the week

Monday	hétfő
Tuesday	kedd
Wednesday	szerda
Thursday	csütörtök
Friday	péntek
Saturday	szombat
Sunday	vasárnap

Time

today	ma
yesterday	tegnap
tomorrow	holnap
day	nap
week	hét
month	hónap
year	év

Basic phrases

yes/no	igen/nem
please	kérem (kérek)
you're welcome	szívesen
Thank you	köszönöm
(very much)	(szépen)
bon appetit!	egészégére!
hello/goodbye	(informal) szia!
goodbye	viszontlátásra
good morning	jó reggelt
good day	jó napot
good evening	jó estét
good night	jó éjszakat
small/large	kicsi, kis/nagy
quickly/slowly	gyorsan/lassan
cold/hot	hideg/meleg
left/right	balra/jobbra
straight ahead	egyenesen előre
where?	hol?
when?	mikor?
why?	miért?
open	nyitva
closed	zárva
how much?	mennyibe kerül?
expensive/cheap	drága/olcsó

Candidate for modernisation – the Post Office

PUBLIC TRANSPORT

Public transport (see pages 22–3) is cheap and efficient. It is strongly recommended to buy a whole-day ticket (*Napijegy*), a three-day one (*Háromnapos jegy*) or a weekly pass (*Hetijegy*), valid on all forms of transport. A monthly pass (*Havijegy*) requires a photograph. All season tickets are available at the ticket office of the larger metro stations. Individual journey tickets must be validated in the punches on trams, trolley buses, the yellow metro and at the entrance to the stations of the other metro lines.

Public transport runs between 4 or 5am and around 11pm, but there are night routes (marked with É on the stops concerned) for some buses and trams. HÉV suburban trains are useful for visiting Szentendre (see pages 132–3) and Ráckeve (see pages 138–9). Tickets for Budapest transport are valid on HÉV lines as far as the city boundary.

Taxis

The most reliable and economic are: **Fötaxi** (tel: 222–2222), **Volántaxi** (tel: 166–6666) and **City Taxi** (tel: 211–1111). Avoid freelancers.

TELEPHONES

For long distance calls within Hungary dial 06, followed by the district code and number. For calls abroad first dial 00 to get an international line. The international operator is 09. Country codes: **Australia** 61, **Ireland** 353, **New Zealand** 64, **UK** 44, **USA** and **Canada** 1.

Phonecards are available from post offices, but cannot be used in all booths. Budapest's formerly catastrophic telephone system has now undergone extensive modernisation.

The Thomas Cook Traveltalk Card is a pre-paid telephone card supported by 24-hour multi-lingual customer service. Available from Thomas Cook branches in the UK in £10 and £20 denominations, the card can be re-charged by calling the customer service unit and quoting your credit card number.

TIME

Hungary is one hour ahead of GMT (Greenwich Mean Time), six hours ahead of EST (Eastern Standard Time) and nine ahead of PST (Pacific Standard Time). Add one hour for summer time (April to September).

TIPPING

Porters, maids, cloakroom attendants,

guides, garage attendants, waiters and gypsy violinists will all expect tips of between 100 and 500Ft. There are no hard and fast rules but 10–15 per cent is standard for waiters and taxi drivers. The custom is to tip at the same time as paying.

TOILETS

There are plenty of public toilets in Budapest. As elsewhere most in cafés, restaurants or hotels tend to be cleaner. Leave a few *forints* in the saucer by the

door. Signs – *mosdó* (WC); *férfi* (men); *női* (women).

TOURIST INFORMATION

Everything you want to know about travel and events in Budapest and Hungary can be answered by TOURINFORM, Sütő utca 2, (50m from Deák Ferenc tér metro), tel: 117–9800, open daily from 8am to 8pm. The friendly staff are multilingual. Note that it is not a booking office.

BUDAPEST METRO

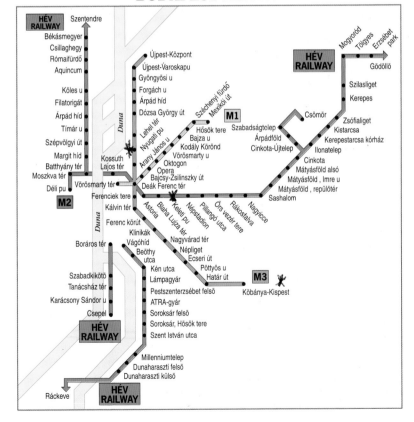

ACKNOWLEDGEMENTS

The Automobile Association wishes to thank the following organisations, libraries and photographers for their assistance in the preparation of this book.

ARDEA LONDON 159b; **CLIVE BARDA/P.A.L.** 70/1, 70, 71; **HUNGARIAN NATIONAL MUSEUM** 63; **HUNGARIAN TOURIST BOARD** 16; **MAGNUM PHOTOS LTD** 10, 11a, 11b, 11c (Erich Lessing); **NATIONAL GALLERY OF HUNGARY** 41; **SPECTRUM COLOUR LIBRARY** cover
The remaining pictures are held in the AA Photo Library and were taken by Ken Paterson with the exception of spine and pages 13, 23, 26, 31, 127b, which were taken by Eric Meacher, and inset (cover), 8, 21, 27, 50b, 73, 131, 138, 166, 176, 184 which were taken by Peter Wilson.

CONTRIBUTORS
Series adviser: Melissa Shales   **Copy editor:** Audrey Horne   **Indexer:** Marie Lorimer
Thanks to **Louis James** for his updating work on this revised edition.